FIVE LESSONS
FOR
LEARNING FROM LOSS

A RESOURCE FOR MOURNERS

AND

HANDBOOK FOR PROVIDERS OF HELP

FIVE LESSONS
FOR
LEARNING FROM LOSS

A RESOURCE FOR MOURNERS
AND
HANDBOOK FOR PROVIDERS OF HELP

JAMES R. DAVIS
AND
JULIE DAVIS ROBINSON

SUNSTONE PRESS

SANTA FE

© 2025 by James R. Davis
All Rights Reserved
No part of this book may be reproduced in any form or by any electronic or mechanical means including
information storage and retrieval systems without permission in writing from the publisher,
except by a reviewer who may quote brief passages in a review.

Sunstone books may be purchased for educational, business, or sales promotional use.
For information please write: Special Markets Department, Sunstone Press,
P.O. Box 2321, Santa Fe, New Mexico 87504-2321.
Printed on acid-free paper
∞
eBook: 978-1-61139-790-1

LIBRARY OF CONGRESS CATALOGING IN PUBLICATION DATA

(ON FILE)

WWW.SUNSTONEPRESS.COM
SUNSTONE PRESS / POST OFFICE BOX 2321 / SANTA FE, NM 87504-2321 /USA
(505) 988-4418

Dedication

We dedicate this book to the loved ones we have lost. With fond memories, we cherish their continuing impact on our lives.

CONTENTS

PREFACE

Everyone dies eventually, some surprisingly sooner or later than expected, through "natural" causes or tragic circumstances, such as accidents, menacing storms, or acts of violence; but in each case, someone is left behind coping with that loss. Although most people are resilient and go on with life, the process of adaptation and living with loss is often very painful. It is also an opportunity for learning.

This book is for people who have experienced a loss through the death of someone close and are learning to adjust to what is often a rather horrible experience. This is a resource for mourners, but it is also a handbook for providers of help: counselors, grief educators, healthcare professionals, social workers, and clergy—anyone who hopes to be of some assistance in the process called grieving, including a neighborhood friend. We sometimes refer to providers informally in this book as *helpers*.

LEARNING WITH THIS BOOK

Learning about loss is the necessary first step toward coping as well as helping. The chapters of this book contain five lessons for learning from loss that can be used to structure a grief workshop, as guidelines for counseling sessions, as material for informal discussions by healthcare staff and clergy, or simply as a resource for the mourner who is learning about loss alone, at their own pace, and in their own way.

The lessons are carefully structured to bring together important information available in key studies of the grief process and to put that information into a usable format. Interspersed with that information are checklists, questions, scales, and activities that help apply that knowledge in an organized and systematic way to the individual who is coping with loss. For example, in Lesson One, the common assertion, "everyone's grief is different' is not just repeated, as it often is, but is explained through a careful analysis of the type of relationship it was, its nature, strength and length, and the surrounding circumstances of the loss, so that the person left behind can gain perspective on the unique loss they are experiencing and what impact certain factors are likely to have on their grief.

In addition to an orderly exploration of the type and nature of the loss in Lesson 1, we include in the other lessons suggestions for constructing and telling the stories of what happened and expressing the varied feelings associated with loss. Methods for working on the tasks of grieving are presented, and activities that may be helpful in coping with loss are described. Suggestions for adapting to a new life are explored, and the difficult timeless questions that arise from loss are examined. Scattered throughout the lessons at appropriate points are poignant short quotations from poets, novelists, and non-fiction authors describing in a touching and enlightening way some aspect of their own grief. Each lesson also contains dialogues between a counselor and a mourner who has experienced grief, intended as illustrations of the ideas covered in each lesson. Detailed but readable analysis, therefore, is accompanied by the sharing of authentic personal experiences, feelings, and emotional challenges that the authors know well. One might say, this is a book written from the head and the heart.

Literature on Grief

A large and varied literature on grief exists, and in recent years some illuminating research has begun to emerge. It appears that the literature can be divided into reports of research studies with instruments and scales used, books with extensive case studies, textbooks for counselors and therapists, self-help books for the bereaved, memoirs based on an individual experience, and literary descriptions of loss. The research studies are important for dispelling unfounded assertions and establishing foundational knowledge about the actual process of grieving as it is presently understood. Self-help books and case studies vary considerably in their usefulness to a particular reader, from vivid descriptions filled with examples of adjustment, to daily spiritual meditations.

Memoirs—sometimes the work of celebrities—are usually descriptive of a particular personal loss and may or may not be generalizable to a reader's own situation.

Famous authors have also written profound and beautiful descriptions about death and loss. Brief quotations of these descriptions are drawn from the carefully documented collection by Mary Jane Moffatt entitled *In the Midst of Winter: Selections from the Literature of Mourning*. One exceptional textbook in its Fifth Edition is *Grief Counseling and Grief Therapy* by the Harvard scholar J. William Worden. It is an important and comprehensive resource of current research literature and basic concepts, although as a technical textbook for training grief therapists, it may not reach those suffering a painful loss or busy frontline professionals providing help.

Eleven books have been selected as "most helpful" to the writing of this book, including Moffat's collection and Worden's text, and these are listed and described at the end of this book in the Annotated Bibliography. One of the main purposes of this work is to translate into usable form the research findings and concepts that appear in the foundational literature on grief developed by respected scholars.

Definitions

What is *loss*? Many forms of loss exist, including loss of a home or certain cherished possessions, loss of one's job, loss of a spouse through divorce or separation, loss of a friend who moves away, and loss of children who leave behind an "empty nest." We define loss more narrowly, for the purpose of this book, as the loss that comes through the death of a family member, partner, or close friend. Sometimes the person who has experienced loss is referred to as *bereaved*, a person suffering the death of a loved one.

What is *learning from loss*? Perhaps learning is a low priority for someone suffering intensely from a loss. Mourners surely don't want to take a test on grieving. The learning involved here is not just about the process of grieving, although there is much to learn about that, but also the more general learning about ourselves, wherever we are in life, that can come about as a response to loss. Loss often includes a lot of suffering and confusion, but also certain opportunities for learning more about life and death, our own lives, and the mysteries of life in general. Maybe our loved ones would be pleased if they knew we are not only adapting to our loss but also trying to learn from it as we live on.

Worden's text is a valuable resource for defining the terminology that is used throughout this book. What is *grief*? Grief is usually referred to as the experience of a person who has suffered a loss. The emphasis is usually on what that person feels and how the response to those feelings is developed through various *tasks*, sometimes referred to as *grief work*. When the grieving process is terminated too quickly through a quick remarriage or sudden change, it is referred to as *abbreviated grief*. Sometimes when grief continues unresolved, causing further upset in a person's life to the point of some personal dysfunction, it is called *complicated grief*, and the person may need extended treatment to be able to return to a more normal life. *Disenfranchised grief* is the term used for grief that is not socially sanctioned, as in the case of an illicit love affair, or when the loss is very difficult to talk about, as with HIV/AIDS or suicide. Sometimes the grief experienced from the loss of a pet is referred to as disenfranchised grief, because some would say it shouldn't be compared to human loss even though the feelings of loss may be very similar.

Mourning usually refers to the broader process of what people do in response to a loss and may include wearing special clothing or making arrangements to remember or memorialize the person who has been lost. The person who plans and carries out these activities is often referred to as a *mourner*. But mourning also appears to include the broader tasks of *grieving*, the process of working through the feelings associated with loss and discovering a new way to live. Although the words to describe the response to a loss have slightly different meanings, they are often used interchangeably, particularly *grieving* and *mourning*.

THE AUTHORS

The co-authors of this book are a father and daughter team, the father being a retired professor and the daughter a licensed and practicing psychologist. You can learn more about us in the Authors section at the back of this book. Although the father has done much of the research, conceptualizing, and writing of the first drafts, the daughter has had a critical eye in the editing process and helping to shape the dialogues. We smile sometimes at the parental role reversal in our writing relationship. The daughter's early years of refining her writing skills by seeking editing help and approval from her dad contrast with her new-found role of suggesting revisions to her father, who now seeks *her* approval of *his* drafts.

The examples discussed in the dialogues come from what may be the father's somewhat unusual experience of loss: a grandfather, mother and father, sister and brother, blind and handicapped daughter, first wife, colleague, and more recently a beloved spouse. The first wife, who died at age forty-two from a type of cancer known as lymphoma, was the co-author daughter's mother. The father's deceased disabled daughter was also her sister. Yes, as mourners, we are acquainted with grief.

In the dialogues, however, we have chosen to take on separate roles distinct from father and daughter. As the father becomes the mourner, sharing aspects of his real-life experiences with loss, the daughter crafts a counselor, perhaps we could say an imagined counselor, who is the skilled listener that converses with the mourner, asking the right questions and responding with empathy and discreet challenges as a counselor would. The goal of the dialogue sections is to illustrate the ideas presented in each lesson and to model how helpers can help.

DIALOGUE

Counselor: How was it that you decided to delve into writing a book on grief in your retirement?

Mourner: After losing so many loved ones, I have a heightened sense of how precious life is. It is important to me to use my time wisely. I decided that I wanted to describe for others what I had experienced personally. Then I began reading more about grief to discover what scholars are saying about it today. My brain started to create ideas for a book, and I began to write.

Counselor: Did it add to the sadness of your own mourning to read those books on grief and think so much about loss?

Mourner: Well, yes, somewhat, but sadness is there for those who suffer loss. I can't make it go away, but I can learn to adapt to it. And I have been greatly assisted by many providers of help, by a supportive grief group, and now by my extensive reading. I've learned a lot, and what does a teacher do with learning?

Counselor: You feel a need to share it? Create lessons for mourners as well as those providing help to the bereaved?

Mourner: Yes. If there is anything that I can contribute through this book that will ease the pain of mourning and help people learn from their loss, that's what I want to do. Maybe it's also a type of memorial to all those loved ones I've lost.

Counselor: Well, making memorials is an important part of mourning.

Mourner: My grief group still meets after two and a half years. One day, one of the members said, "We all seem to know something that other people don't know. Isn't that so?" We all nodded solemnly. We had learned from the intensity of our loss about the importance of life.

LESSON 1

DEFINING PERSONAL LOSS AND UNDERSTANDING THE CIRCUMSTANCES IMPACTING GRIEF

The first few days of the initial experience of loss and the earliest weeks of grief are filled with intense and sometimes agonizing feelings. Usually, the person who suffered the loss simply needs and wants an understanding listener. Telling the story of one's loss is the subject of Lesson Two, including guidance on what feelings are likely to surface and ways to express them. We want to acknowledge at the beginning of this lesson that the early weeks of grief may be filled with such intense and disruptive feelings that the person experiencing them may not care about anything but describing what happened and being understood.

It may be valuable, however, if it is possible, to try to step back from those feelings briefly and explore carefully what this loss really is, who it involved, and what the relationship was between the person who was lost and the one remaining alive. The opportunity for systematic reflection on the nature of the loss, presented in this lesson, is an important starting point for discovering what the loss is, seeing it in a broader context, and exploring how the grief process is likely to be impacted in each instance.

Many factors can influence the nature, intensity, and duration of grief. J. William Worden refers to these influences as "mediators" of grief. (Worden, 2018, Chapter 3) Those who conduct research refer to them as variables. Mediators exhibit indirect causation, connection, or relation. In any case, it is very important to understand how a wide range of factors can influence the grief being experienced. Although it is difficult to predict exactly what influence these mediating factors will have or how strong their influence will be, common sense suggests that mourning for a teenage son or daughter suddenly lost in a school shooting may be different from the anticipated loss of a grandparent from natural causes. Mediators of grief are important to identify because at some point they will have a direct or indirect impact on the shape and tasks of mourning. As Worden explains, "Mourning behavior is multidetermined." (Worden, 2918, p.76) One good reason for considering mediating factors carefully is to try to identify which mourners may be at high risk for complicated and prolonged grief. Who may have an especially difficult time?

IDENTIFYING THE RELATIONSHIP

Much of the writing about grief stresses that every loss is different, but there is seldom a discussion of why. By reading this chapter and completing the suggested activities, a better understanding can be developed of the way every loss is unique and how one's own loss can be described and better understood. First, we need to ask who died, and what was their relationship to the persons who are still alive, sometimes referred to as kinship. (Worden, 2018, Chapter 3) That is a significant first step toward understanding why every loss is different. A list of kinship relationships is provided in Figure 1. Mourners may wish to review the list and check the descriptor of the person or persons who died.

KINSHIP RELATIONSHIPS

From this list of possible relationships, check the kinship relationship of the person who died.

___ grandparent

___ father or mother

___ sister or brother

___ spouse or partner

___ child

___ in-law

___ stepfamily member

___ close friend

___ work associate

___ other ______________________

It should be possible to check just one descriptor. Some people may think that a spouse is also a close friend, but for purposes of identification, it is best to check only one.

Already, we can see that the kinship relationship itself is likely to have a significant impact on the nature of the loss. Why?

A *grandparent* usually involves a more distant relationship, unless of course, that grandparent served as a parent in raising the child. Sometimes geographic distance keeps grandparents from being better known. But losing a grandparent, with some understandable exceptions, is different from losing a parent or spouse.

Losing a *parent* is usually not the same as losing a grandparent because the relationship is usually much closer and may have a feature of dependency. The parental relationship, however, is sometimes filled with contradiction and conflict. Our parents "raise" us, which involves not only support, security, and love, but telling us (at least at an early age) what we can and cannot do and even punishing us for our behavior. Children who dearly love and respect their parents have probably at one time or another also rebelled against them. The task of becoming an adult also involves breaking away from parents to find one's own identity and pathway. The role of parent invites built-in confusion for grieving children.

The loss of a *sister* or *brother* can vary widely depending on age, geographic proximity, and degree of liking. Siblings are noted for "rivalry" as well as caring as they are growing up, and that relationship can be respectful or fraught with mixed feelings in later life.

Losing a *spouse* is inherently different from losing a grandparent, parent, or sibling. Spouses (or partners) usually live together closely, with many opportunities for attachment and affection as well as disagreement and conflict. Whether the relationship was satisfying or not, it was close, marked by the intimacy and intensity of living together that makes it unique.

Losing a *child* can happen at any point from infancy through later adulthood and is also marked by inherent contradiction: parents are "supposed" to die before children, and having a child die before a parent can be upsetting and confusing for both. Because the parental role (at its best) involves unconditional love, it may lead to strong attachment to the child and difficult grief. The loss of a child, more common in earlier generations, is still very difficult at any age. This also includes the death of unborn children and newly born children and the loss of hopes and dreams their parents had for them. The loss of a stillborn child, the loss from Sudden Infant Death Syndrome (SIDS), or the losses associated with miscarriage or abortion (Worden, 2018, pp. 195-203) are often left out of the discussion, perhaps as disenfranchised grief. But such losses may also be very painful and create a need for mourning. The author Charles Lamb, 1775–1834, wrote these words in *On an Infant Dying as Soon as Born,* as cited in Moffat, 1992, p. 79.

> A flo'ret crushed in the bud,
> A nameless piece of babyhood,
> Was in her cradle coffin lying;
> Extinct with scarce sense of dying
> So soon to exchange the imprisoned womb
> For darker closets of the tomb!

In-laws (brother, sister, mother, or father-in-law) are usually not part of the immediate family, and relationships can be either close or distant. Usually, however, losing a brother-in-law or sister-in-law is not quite like losing a brother or sister. Likewise with parental in-laws. They all arrive later in a person's life, after marriage, official or not.

Stepfamily relationships develop when a remarriage has taken place and parents, children and siblings play roles that are different from "blood" relationships. Often these are referred to as "blended families." Feelings can vary in strength, but they will almost assuredly be different in stepfamilies.

Sometimes a loss can affect an entire family system and grief is experienced differently by different members of the family. A loss can cause disruptions in the way families interact as a unit. (Worden, 2018, p. 218)

Often a *friend,* technically not kin, becomes as close as or even closer than a family member. Friends are chosen, family members (except for a spouse) are not, and having chosen, cultivated, and nourished a friendship over a period of time, one can experience a significant sense of loss when that person dies.

Work associates are people who have become essential colleagues and sometimes just good friends. Often, they can also be close, and their loss may be upsetting. Some people spend a significant amount of time together at work.

Other relationships, not described above, may exist, and these may also be experienced as loss upon death. Our guess is that many people who might check this option may be thinking of a pet. Because this type of loss is somewhat misunderstood when discussing grief, we left "pet loss" off the official list, but we will discuss it later in this lesson and in others.

The relationships described here involve roles, not the word's first meaning, which is an actor's part in a play or film, but a person's function in a particular relationship that may carry with it certain expectations or responsibilities, such as father and daughter, sister and brother. Both the deceased and the survivors have usually played roles that have affected their relationship, and these can influence the loss and the grief. Roles affect relationships and relationships affect grief associated with loss.

DESCRIBING THE NATURE AND QUALITY OF THE RELATIONSHIP

After identifying the relationship, it is important to ask some questions about the nature and quality of that relationship. Was this a close or distant relationship? Was it happy or stressful? Was it intense or casual? The chart at the end of this section can be used to help describe and summarize the unique relationship with the person who has been lost.

CLOSE OR DISTANT

Sometimes the closeness of a relationship is partially defined by geography: people separated by distance don't have the opportunity to develop a close relationship because they don't see each other very often. On the other hand, a close relationship may have developed earlier in life, and the geographical distance that came later is experienced as disruptive. Closeness, however, usually refers to emotional closeness or liking, not proximity.

Authors who describe close relationships often use the word *attachment*. (Worden, 2018, Chapter 3) This is a term that became popular in referring to the bonding of a mother and infant child, and it usually refers to the love and security that the mother provides and the trust and dependence evoked in the child. When applied to adult relationships, such as with a spouse, attachment refers to the emotional involvement people have for each other, their degree of bonding and caring. Love may be a word that is too strong or general, but attachment surely involves liking. It also (usually) implies some degree of liking that is reciprocal. It is possible, of course, for a parent to be more attached than a child is in return, or for a brother to like his sister more than she likes him. But in general, liking is mutual. As Worden notes, strong attachment is noticeable also in animals (geese and dolphins) as well as in humans. Attachment is also strong between humans and pets, and pets with their owners. (Nieburg and Fischer, 1982) When the attachment is close, sometimes very close, the grief process will be more difficult compared to a relationship that might be described as distant. Research on attachment is relatively recent, but feelings of attachment and loss are reflected in these lines from a fourth century, CE, Chinese poet P'An Yuch, drawn from *In Mourning for His Dead Wife,* as cited in Moffatt, pp. 119-120.

> She vanishes. And I
> Am overwhelmed with sorrow.
> Two birds made a nest and then
> There was only one. A pair
> Of fishes were separated.

HAPPY OR STRESSFUL

Relationships can be calm, smooth, and happy, or filled with frequent disagreements producing considerable stress. Anger may be expressed openly and frequently or held in check, swimming beneath the surface; but when the relationship is unhappy, it can be stressful for those who are part of it. Open hostilities are troublesome, but so are cold wars where differences are unspoken and avoided instead of addressed and resolved. When someone dies amid stressful relationships, grief can be accompanied by guilt or regret, or even additional hostile behavior. Positive relationships are preferred for happy living, but a loss involving a happy relationship can also be extremely painful. It is important to know whether grief is difficult because it involves disruption of a happy relationship, or whether it has become difficult because of a stressful relationship preceding the loss. Degrees of stress and happiness are mediators and will affect grief.

Intense or Casual

How intense or casual was the relationship with the person who died? Sometimes spouses who truly care about each other can go through life together casually side by side with great respect for each other but not much intensity. The relationship is solid and caring, but there is seldom strong emotion that goes with it. The relationship is casual, and both parties prefer it that way, or the relationship is full of intense emotions, and both are happy with that. Sometimes casual parents back off, giving their children the freedom to become themselves and do as they wish. Others, sometimes known as "helicopter parents," are intensely involved in their children's lives, monitoring closely what they read and listen to, while watching every detail as they raise them in their preferred manner. Likewise, some siblings may have an intense relationship with one brother or sister, while casually ignoring the others.

There is probably no optimal level of intensity, but each relationship will have some degree of it that may affect grief. Many children will have a casual relationship with a grandparent, unless they were orphaned as children and raised by an intense "helicopter grandparent." In other words, intensity depends on circumstances, but also on the personalities and values of those involved. Some people grow intensely excited over small matters while others remain casual about very important ones. Intense relationships may lead to deeper and longer mourning. More casual relationships may lead to quiet gratitude or occasional regret. Either way, the intensity of the relationship is likely to affect grief.

Influential or Low Impact

Some people say that "opposites attract," but others will say, "they were like two peas in a pod," meaning they were very similar in almost every way. People who are different can still have a strong impact on each other. Someone who is very quiet may appreciate having an outgoing spouse or sibling to do the talking or help bring them out. People who are similar, on the other hand, can also have a strong influence, reinforcing their common interests in sports, music, cooking or literature. In both cases the influence of one upon the other can have a high or low impact. The strength of influence in the relationship may affect the grief process.

In relationships where the participants have a strong influence on each other, it tends to impact what some psychologists call the "self." (Hagman, 2016, Chapter 8) Although there is some disagreement about whether there is such a thing as a permanent or on-going self, most would agree that at the time of death, each person has something that might be called a self. The two selves in a relationship may have been somewhat independent, not affecting the other very much, or they may have become quite intertwined or enmeshed through strong influence and interdependence. When one person dies within a relationship where both have been influenced strongly by the other, the person left behind may say, "It feels like I lost part of myself." Ralph Waldo Emerson, 1803-1882, American poet and essayist, put it this way in *Threnody,* as cited in Moffat, 1992, p.65.

> The eager fate which carried thee
> Took the largest part of me.

In high impact relationships like that, grief may be strongly affected. Reflecting on losing a part of the self and building a new self, as described further in Lesson 4, can be important parts of grieving. Relationships can be described as having a high or low impact and can affect the grief related to such a loss.

CLEAR OR AMBIGUOUS

Sometimes a relationship is close, happy, and influential. A different relationship might be perceived as distant, stressful, and casual with little impact. But in each case, to those involved, the relationship may seem clear. They know what to expect, their behavior is consistent, and surprises don't happen often. In other relationships, however, things are not so clear, maybe even muddy, foggy, and hard to describe. Love and hate may exist side by side. (Worden, 2018, p. 70) The relationship might be quite happy one day, but very stressful on another, or things might be casual for several weeks, and then an intense, angry exchange explodes. It becomes difficult to know what will happen next.

Relationships where behavior is mixed are often called ambiguous, that is, having more than one possible meaning, unclear and puzzling. We are led to the related word, ambivalence, to describe the way a person might have mixed feelings about a relationship like that. It can happen in many different relationships, including spouses, parents and children, and siblings. Mixed feelings predominate, such as respect mixed with disgust, or caring mixed with annoyance, and then someone in that relationship dies. The esteemed French writer Marcel Proust, 1871-1972, described his mixed feelings about his father in this prose passage from his *Letters*, as cited in Moffatt, 1992, p.181.

> You, who saw father only two or three times, have no way of knowing how kind and simple he was. I tried—if not exactly to satisfy him for I am well aware that I was always the disappointment of his life—at least to show him my affection.

It seems that grieving grows more difficult when there is ambivalence. Sorrow is sometimes mixed with relief, respect with regret, and affection with shame. Because ambivalence makes things confusing for those involved, it is hard to predict exactly what will happen with grief, but chances are that the grief associated with such relationships can be intricate or convoluted. For example, a caregiver may feel both relief and a sense of emptiness at the lost role of caregiver, as well as deep sadness upon losing a loved one. The strong feelings of an already mixed-up situation become thrown together with the feelings of grief, so a person is never quite sure what to feel about this loss. It may take more time to separate and examine mixed feelings.

CHARTING THE RELATIONSHIP

After identifying the relationship, it is important to reflect on the nature and quality of that relationship because it will probably affect the grieving process related to that loss. How is the relationship with the person who died most accurately described? Mourners may summarize the nature of the relationship by completing the chart in Figure 2.

FIGURE 2

CHARTING THE RELATIONSHIP

Place a checkmark somewhere along the line between the two words to describe the type of relationship it was. Do this for each of the pairs of words. A check near to Close indicates a close relationship, and a check near to Distant indicates a more distant relationship. A check in the middle means sometimes Close and sometimes Distant, or perhaps somewhat Close, but not really Distant.

Close _______________________	Distant
Happy _______________________	Stressful
Intense _______________________	Casual
Influential _______________________	Low Impact
Clear _______________________	Ambiguous

When death has come and involves the relationship described in this chart, the grieving may vary considerably depending on the nature and quality of the relationship. This explains partly why every loss is different and every grief is different. It is clearly an individual matter and many mediators influence the grief that is experienced. But other factors also influence that difference, such as the duration of the relationship, the cause of death, and the personal characteristics and outlooks of the person who has experienced the loss. We will explore these as well.

DURATION OF THE RELATIONSHIP

How long was the relationship now disrupted by loss? Some spouses have celebrated their fiftieth wedding anniversary; others may have been married for only a few months before something tragic happened to one of them. A parent dies of natural causes after age eighty, while another dies of cancer leaving young children behind. The age of the deceased and the length of the relationship can affect loss and grief.

The age of the persons (usually more than one) who have experienced the loss also affects grief and mourning. Age usually reflects a stage in life, and this, not the mere number marking one's age, is what matters. A child of ten losing a parent prematurely is a rather different situation from a grown child of sixty losing a parent in their eighties. Parents in their thirties losing a six-month-old infant experience something different from adult and aging parents losing a fifty-year-old child from cancer. Siblings don't always die in their precise birth order, and an early death of the youngest can be unusually upsetting for the others. Friends may be of similar ages, and an unanticipated loss of one of them can be disturbing. All of these situations, defined by age, can influence grief.

At what stage in the mourner's life has the loss come? One of the pioneers in delineating and explaining developmental stages is Erik Erikson. (Erikson 1968) Building on his work, Daniel Levinson studied people of all ages and by asking them what they were focused on, he was able to lay out an empirically based set of stages that fit numerical age. (Levinson, 1978, 1996) After childhood and the identity formation of adolescence, he saw a turning point which he called age thirty transition, and then another in the mid-life between age forty and forty-three when people seem to be evaluating everything in their life and either commit to continuing as things are or making important changes. Older people focus on their legacy and life review. The way in which a mourner responds to a loss depends to some extent on whether they are a child, an adolescent, a young person just starting out in life, someone in mid-life who is tending to reevaluate everything, or an elderly person. The way an older person responds to the death of a spouse may be affected by their own sense of approaching mortality. Those who have experienced loss may vary considerably in their ability to focus on mourning, their interest in it, their time for it, and the importance it has to them at that stage of their life. The result may be *abbreviated grief.* Harsh as it may sound, people don't always have time for mourning, being occupied with other aspects of their life, but when it is neglected, at least in some cases where troublesome issues have not been resolved, consequences may appear later in life. George Hagman refers to this as "arrested mourning," or unresolved mourning that leads, in a limited number of cases to pathological outcomes that my need later resolution. (Hagman, 2016, Chapter 6)

It is important to consider the age of the deceased and the ages of the primary mourners to get a sense of how these differences and similarities may affect the experience of grief. A mourner may wish to write down these ages and ponder what they might mean, including how long the mourners have known the deceased.

CAUSE OF DEATH

Almost all loss is painful, but some losses can become even more painful depending on the cause of death. This is also an important mediator that can affect the grieving process. We will begin with natural causes and work our way, painfully, through other circumstances.

Most people, it might be said, die of old age and *natural causes.* This does not make the loss less significant, but the term "natural causes" means at least, that it is anticipated. Unfortunately, even an anticipated loss, one that everyone knows is coming, is often still experienced as a shock when it actually occurs. No one lives forever and everyone dies of something, so natural causes may also include serious diseases, organ malfunction, and disability. The defining characteristic of this kind of death is not the terminal illness, but the degree of inevitability, foreknowledge, and anticipation that comes with it. Caregivers may get deeply involved in a death even from natural causes and may find their efforts to be ineffective, discouraging, and exhausting. Not everyone who dies of natural causes remains lucid and cooperative. Some have serious dementia and others have mental stress that affects attitude and willingness or capacity to cooperate. No loss is easy, but death from natural causes at least has some element of anticipation and expectation.

Sometimes death comes through a *disruptive illness* that precedes the age of normal life expectancy. It can occur at any of life's stages prior to old age, and it is a form of loss that is also anticipated, but it is somehow out-of-place, premature, or contrary to normal expectations of longevity. Because the person is usually younger, their will and strength for survival may be strong, and they are able to live with their disruptive illness for months and even years, sometimes surprisingly. At other times, death may be sudden, as with a stroke or heart attack. Although this death, depending on the nature and severity of the illness, may also be expected, its key feature is its unpredictability. How? When? How long? How much suffering will be involved? These become common and disturbing questions for caregivers. The element of untimeliness also increases the number and depth of questions about the meaning of the illness. How could this happen to such a healthy person? Could it have been prevented? Why does this random death come now? These questions are especially common in the fatal illness of a child. Caregiving for a disruptive illness can also be discouraging and exhausting with heightened worry about so many unknowns. When the loss occurs, the normal suffering of grief may be coupled with unanswerable questions about an untimely death.

Some deaths are *accidental*. Auto accidents come to mind because there are so many of them, but these deaths can also occur in sports activities, such as asphyxiation in an avalanche while skiing, drowning in a boating or diving accident, or a fatal fall in mountain climbing. They also occur increasingly in the *natural disasters* of fire, tornado, flood, hurricane, earthquake, or tsunami, all of which seem to be increasingly deadly. They may sometimes involve a victim's suffering over time, but usually these deaths are sudden and unexpected, often leaving those who remain alive in a state of shock and denial. Overdose deaths may be accidental or suicidal, sometimes making the cause of death ambiguous. Accidental deaths are often dramatic, sometimes filled with horror and many "what if" questions. What if they had taken a different route? Why did they go that day? Why wasn't there more warning? Why did it happen there? Usually, an accidental death leads to strong, confusing, and perhaps angry emotions of grief.

Death from a *homicide,* a murder of some kind, is increasingly common, and the rates fluctuate up and down. Domestic violence homicides, growing out of personal or family disagreements are frequent, but drive-by shootings, road rage murders, and mass shootings are now common. Particularly disturbing are mass murders of children in school shootings. Sometimes homicides grow out of disagreements between people known to each other, and perhaps have grown to dislike each other, while other murders are anonymous, though still filled with hate based on skin color, ethnic background, or sexual preference. Mass murders are usually random, where victims are not known by those who have killed them. The feeling associated with accidental death are there, but a sense of horror and absurdity magnify the grief associated with homicides.

The frequency of *military deaths* depends on the extent of involvement in actual warfare, though training deaths occur occasionally. Military deaths are shocking because of the potential violence to the human body, and survivors are left with a sense of horror and uncertainty over how the death may have occurred, if that is even known. The culture of the soldier's country usually makes military deaths seem to be for a good cause and even heroic, making mourning confusing. It may have been heroic, but it is a loss, and grief is likely to include anger, regret, and even defiance mixed with pride. Usually, the mourner is left with many questions: How did this happen? Who is responsible? Could it have been prevented? Heroic military deaths may seem like the result of a mistake or misfortune that cannot be explained. Mourning often involves obligatory memorials.

Death from *suicide* is an especially troubling loss. People who are overcome by problems so intense that they are driven to take their own life may or may not be able to imagine the problems they have left behind for their survivors. In addition to all the usual factors that influence the nature and quality of the relationship, a choice has been made to end the relationship with key survivors, leaving them with a special kind of loss that is confusing, painful, and full of a sense of responsibility and almost inevitable guilt. The normal feelings of grief are confused by regret. What went wrong? Was this preventable?

Worden reports that traumatic deaths (accidents, suicides, and homicides) are frequently associated with more intense grief. Especially difficult are "troubling images" related to finding or visualizing the body. (Worden, 2018, p.63)

Knowing the cause of death, to the extent that it can be known, provides perspective on how that loss will affect grief. If every loss is unique, understanding the cause of death will add to that sense of uniqueness, but more importantly, it will be a warning signal of what to watch for in the grieving process. All loss is difficult to understand and cope with, but some grief may be more painful and intense because of the cause of death. A checklist of the causes of death appears in Figure 3.

Figure 3

Causes of Death

What kind of death was this? Check the description that best applies. What are the implications for mourning?

_____ natural causes

_____ disruptive illness

_____ accident

_____ natural disaster

_____ homicide

_____ military

_____ suicide

Likely implications: ______________________________________

____

Sometimes multiple losses occur in one event, such as a traffic accident or natural disaster, in which case mourners with several losses at once may experience *bereavement overload*. (Worden, 2018, p. 63) What would it be like to fill out this checklist for more than one person?

Characteristics of the Mourner

Much emphasis has been placed on the relationship of the mourner to the deceased, but what about the personal characteristics and situation of the mourner? However shocked, upset, or confused by the loss, to what extent is the person who is experiencing it prepared or unprepared to face it? What is their developmental stage in life at the time that the loss occurred? How much disruption will there be and how well are they prepared for it? What are the personal characteristics of the person who has experienced this loss, and how will these affect the grieving process?

Almost no one is "ready" for a loss, but some are better off than others with regard to their circumstances in life. Does the loss create financial difficulties? Will a place of residence be lost, too? Was a will prepared and is insurance in place for a clear transition for beneficiaries? Sometimes a death can produce serious loss of income or unexpected financial upset. Perhaps new responsibilities come for the care and raising of children. At other times, however, there is not much impact on the mourner's situation in life, except for the loss itself.

The daily routines of life and household chores are disrupted because the person who engaged in them is gone. Sometimes when gender roles are sharply defined, the person left behind doesn't know how to do the things that the deceased did, including such diverse things as using technology, managing the finances, cooking, cleaning, doing laundry (indoor chores) or gardening, shoveling snow, or taking care of the car (outdoor chores). New family responsibilities may emerge, such as becoming a single parent responsible for young children or becoming the remaining sibling now in charge of aging parents. All these things may require some adaptation, but usually it is not a difficult response to make, given sufficient time and support. Often these adjustments add to the burden of grief, but sometimes they may facilitate it, giving the mourner new things to learn and do.

The more significant challenge, however, is usually the emotional adjustment, coping with the waves of feeling that can be so strong as to make it difficult to function. What are the characteristics of the individual who experiences the loss, and which of these attributes will help facilitate a positive adjustment, as opposed to leading the mourner down the path to unresolved and complicated grief?

Is the person accustomed to facing feelings and dealing with them, or is there a history of or tendency toward denial and repression? Some people have had to deal with other situations where deep feelings are involved, including previous losses or loss unrelated to death, and they may have already learned to confront their feelings honestly and openly. This may have included some experience with expressing those feelings, either formally with a counselor, with empathetic friends, or even through writing. Having found some comfort in the more general expression of feelings, they may be more able to deal with present grief.

Grief, by its very nature, can lead to uncontrolled expression through crying and sobbing, or to expressing anger or blame, loneliness or sadness. These are all natural and legitimate feelings associated with grief, not only worthy of expression but usually in need of expression, but they can also get out of control and interfere with normal activities and conversations with friends. Some people are more experienced than others in managing their emotions. Mourners also vary in what they believe about locus of control, that is, the ability to control what happens in their life. (Worden, 2018, p.72) Experience in doing so can make a difference in the grieving process.

Attitude, as with almost everything, can be important for grieving. Is the person entering into the experience of grief already gloomy and downcast, a person who tends toward the darker more pessimistic side of life frequently? Or do they have a more positive outlook on life shaped by hope for a better future? Attitude also helps to shape self-concept, the way that people think about themselves and their capabilities. Some people write negative scripts for themselves that become self-fulfilling prophecies. "I'm the kind of person who is disorganized and a bit lazy, and that's just who I am," they say and then they follow the script. Still others may have an unrealistically confident outlook that enables them to believe that they can face any challenge and overcome it alone. Some people are relatively competent at controlling their behavior, facing down temptations, and giving up bad habits, while others may layer grief onto pre-existing mental health disorders. One might ask what concurrent stress is going on in the lives of those who have experienced loss. (Worden, 2018, pp. 75-76) And to what extent are people open to seeking and receiving help, or would they prefer to be left alone?

Let's not judge people for any of these characteristics. We are what we are, and we have been shaped by many experiences and relationships. It is possible to ask, nonetheless, how these characteristics may affect the grieving process. It can be useful for mourners to conduct a short self-assessment of readiness on a variety of personal characteristics as an aid to thinking about what is being brought to the experience of loss. This can be done by completing the assessment in Figure 4.

FIGURE 4

CHARACTERISTICS OF THE MOURNER

Put a check mark somewhere along the continuum from "Ready" to "Unprepared."

| Ready | Unsure | Unprepared |

Financial stability

____

Planned transition

____

Learn new roles

____

Family responsibilities

____

Facing feelings

____

Expressing feelings

____

	Ready	Unsure	Unprepared

Managing emotions

____

Pre-existing disorders

____

Generally positive attitude

____

Healthy self-concept

____

Control of behavior

____

Open to receiving help

____

Thinking through the relationship with the deceased is important for anticipating what grief will be like but so is gaining insight into what is brought to the role of the mourner.

All the mediators of grief described above as characteristics of the relationship of deceased and mourner tend to stress the uniqueness of each person's loss. Although it is important to understand how each loss is different, in sharing a loss, survivors also come to discover that they hold something very much in common through that loss, no matter how different individual circumstances may be. J. William Worden, drawing on an observation by his Harvard professor, the esteemed psychologist, Gordon Allport, concerning his ideas about similarities and differences in the human condition created this thoughtful observation about grief: "Each person's grief is like *all* other people's grief; each person's grief is like *some* other person's grief; and each person's grief is like *no* other person's grief". (Worden, 2018, p.9) An important result from learning about the grief of others, perhaps by sharing that loss informally or through a grief group, is that the bereaved sees quickly that one's unique loss is part of a universal experience of grief that eventually arrives at everyone's doorstep. As the poet, Gerard Manley Hopkins, 1844–1889, has written in *Spring and Fall: To a Young Child,* as cited in Moffat, 1992, p.97.

> No matter, child, the name:
> Sorrows spring the same.

Some of the ideas in this lesson are illustrated in a narrative form in the dialogue that follows between the mourner and a counselor. As mentioned in the Preface, the experiences of the mourner are real, those of the author (father) and retired professor. The counselor is an invented figure, shaped by the co-author (daughter) with her insights as a psychologist in clinical practice.

DIALOGUE

Counselor: You mentioned that you've had many losses. What comes to mind as you think back over these relationships?

Mourner: I lost a grandfather whom I barely knew when I was just a little kid. I don't remember much about that and didn't have any other losses until my wife and mother of my two daughters passed away. She died of lymphoma at age forty-two, which was my age also. That was a horrible experience.

Counselor: So young. You sensed it was coming, but when it happened, it must have been very upsetting.

Mourner: Yes. We were very close in our college age courtship and the early days of our marriage, very happy with a strong common interest in music. She was a gifted pianist. But when our second daughter arrived, our first daughter's younger sister, we were really challenged because she was blind and with cerebral palsy from meningitis, a brain infection, discovered when she was one day old in the hospital.

Counselor: Tell me about the challenges.

Mourner: My wife, and the mother of our handicapped child, had to focus on raising her to be as normal as possible, including helping her to learn to walk through a demanding therapy program staffed by nearly fifty volunteers. So, in a relationship where I had felt very close and happy, I now felt a bit left out. I mean, how can you compete with a handicapped child? And even though my wife did her best, some of the closeness was gone as well as some of the happiness. What had been clear became confusing and a bit ambiguous.

Counselor: Your happy relationship was disrupted.

Mourner: And then again when we learned she had cancer.

Counselor: How long did she have it?

Mourner: For five years, during which she earned another degree and taught yoga and physical fitness classes at the university. She herself was a model of perfect health.

Counselor: And you must have wondered how she could possibly have lymphoma.

Mourner: She did, too. Everyone did. Many friends didn't even know she had it. She was almost in remission at the five-year mark after finishing treatment. Then it came back. She was given six months to live but died within weeks. She died suddenly in the middle of the night at home, and it was a miserable experience for the entire family. How could someone so healthy die that young?

Counselor: How tragic...but some questions seem to have no answers. Then you were left as a single parent of two teen-age daughters, and one was disabled, requiring extra support and care.

Mourner: She had been mostly raised by her mother while I was busy at the university, teaching and writing, and doing consulting to earn a better living for the family.

Counselor: How did you experience the loss?

Mourner: Complete panic! How was I to survive? Okay, my daughter was in school with good special education services, but how was I going to be her mother? And keep an eye out for my older daughter as she headed off to college? I had many new roles and responsibilities, and it was really terrifying.

Counselor: How did you cope?

Mourner: I married my youngest daughter's sixth grade teacher, thinking she would help me out. With only abbreviated grieving for my wife, I rushed into what I only recently have recognized as a "rebound marriage." The loss of my dear wife made me feel completely lost, like I needed help fast. I was kind of out of control emotionally.

Counselor: Your mourning was cut short with your responsibilities?

Mourner: That's a good insight. I think my mother and father mourned her on my behalf. They loved my wife dearly and her death bothered them as if she were their own daughter. In a few years I lost my parents, too, first my mom, who was older, at ninety-two and then my dad at eighty-eight, dying of natural causes. My older brother looked after them, and although I would say I was close and at ease with my parents, we were miles apart, clear across the country from each other. They both had a strong influence on me while I was growing up, and when they were gone, I felt alone in the world, like a grown-up orphan.

Counselor: On your own completely without guidance or security. Do you have siblings?

Mourner: I did. My sister was ten years older than me and died first. We weren't very close, mainly because she left home to get married when I was ten years old. We didn't have much chance to find out if we had anything in common and she was moving all over the country with her husband chasing the American dream. But my brother, that was another matter. He was only seven years older, and as kids we played hardball catch, wrestled on the living room floor, and I played the piano to accompany him on his violin. I visited him a lot back East, at his job through the years, and he had a big influence on my life in a lot of ways.

Counselor: So, you were close as kids and stayed close as adults. Losing him must have been difficult.

Mourner: It was, indeed. We always had good times together. This is a little off the subject, but my brother had a dog, and that dog died while my brother was still alive. My brother was gay, but he had a close female friend, and they lived in a duplex with this dog. When that dog died, it was horrible for both of them. They grieved like that dog was the child they never had.

Counselor: That happens a lot. If I may share, I had a dog that died, too—having to be put down due to old age—and I think I know what you are describing with your brother. A close bond develops with a pet, and the loss can be heart wrenching.

Mourner: Yes, truly. Now I need to tell you what happened with my handicapped daughter. A difficult life of disability apparently wasn't difficult enough, and she had to die in her middle years with horrible suffering from ovarian cancer. I still picture her twisting and turning on her bed, the uncontrollable eyes rolling back, with writhing pain that even strong medication couldn't contain.

Counselor: Oh, dear…so unfair. It must have been awful to watch that. Did it affect your mourning for her?

Mourner: Perhaps I was so disturbed by her suffering that my grief was mostly relief, not for myself, but a special kind of thankfulness that her suffering was at an end. It produced a deep sadness in me, watching her die that way, knowing that her whole life had been so hard. Given her limitations, though, she achieved a lot and had a cheerful disposition and knack for making friends. I remember feeling inspired by her.

Counselor: How so?

Mourner: If a situation required patience, she was patient, if it called for persistence, she was persistent. She finished college and earned a graduate degree. All in Braille.

Counselor: Such a mix of feelings related to your daughter—feeling sad for her about her hardships but also inspired by the way she handled them. Let me see here, I believe you told me you had another loss, more recently. Can you talk about that?

Mourner: I can now, but it was very tough at first. Lots of sobbing. After I was divorced, I met this very wonderful woman in Brazil at a workshop I was conducting. Two people couldn't be more different than we were. She was Brazilian, raised Catholic, and spoke Portuguese as her first language. I was a monolingual American, kind of a Protestant skeptic, and worried about making a new commitment. But she was patient with me, and we both intensely loved classical music, theater, and film, and each other, of course. She was grateful that she could bring her ten-year-old daughter to the US and welcomed me in helping to raise her. She found so many ways to make me happy.

Counselor: It seems like a classic love story. What happened?

Mourner: We were both very close, happy, and intense, and we were a big influence on each other. Everything about that thirty-year relationship was consistently wonderful. We shared everything. We traveled a lot. Our lives were intertwined. Being thirteen years older than she, I thought I would die first, but she had an inherited heart condition, pacemaker and all, so she passed away first. It was a terrible loss for me and the grief associated with that loss was horribly difficult. But I was retired by that time, looking back on a lifetime of accomplishments that should have given me a positive outlook and self-concept. Right? But it is a good thing I was open to receiving help because I really needed it. I fell apart emotionally. I'm still learning from that loss as I write this book. And still grieving for her.

Counselor: That kind of loss is especially difficult.

Mourner: But let me tell you in my remaining minutes about my wife's daughter.

Counselor: That would be your stepdaughter?

Mourner: Yes. She had a lot of family responsibilities at the time her mother died, like I did in my first marriage. She was very busy and dedicated to being a mother herself at the time of her mother's death. She thinks of her mourning as coming and going, off and on, from an out-of-nowhere sudden sobbing reminder that her mom is gone to being caught up in the day-to-day duties of motherhood, with little time to think of anything else but the two daughters.

Counselor: Going from being consumed by grief to being inundated with the responsibilities of family life, so that she could wonder if her grieving was disrupted, similar to the way you told me yours was with your first wife.

Mourner: Possibly, even though the moments of grief, she says, are sometimes very sad and intense for her, too. But she has wonderful ways of remembering her mother. I'll tell you about them later.

Counselor: So in summary, it seems you've had to contend with many different losses.

Mourner: It's a work in progress to put them in perspective.

Counselor: And it seems the losses were all unique, occurring at different stages in your life, which likely had a bearing on how you experienced and adapted to them.

Mourner: True. Yes, the grief was different for each one. I guess that's one lesson I've learned.

REFERENCES

Erickson, E.H. (1968). *Identity Youth and Crisis*. New York: W.W. Norton & Company.

Hagman, G. (Ed.) (2016). *New Models of Bereavement, Theory and Treatment*. New York: Routledge.

Levinson, D.J. (1978). *The Seasons of a Mans' Life*. New York: Alfred A. Knopf.

Levinson, D.J. (1996). *The Seasons of a Woman's Life*. New York: Random House.

Moffat, M.J. (1992). *In the Midst of Winter: Selections from the Literature of Mourning*. New York: Random House.

Nieburgh, H. and Fischer, A. (1982). *Pet Loss*. New York: Harper & Row.

Worden, J.W. (2018). *Grief Counseling and Grief Therapy: A Handbook for Mental Health Practitioners*, Fifth Edition. New York: Springer Publishing.

LESSON 2

TELLING THE STORIES OF WHAT HAPPENED AND DESCRIBING THE FEELINGS OF LOSS

The focus of this lesson is on telling the mourner's story. This usually involves three stories: 1) the life story of the person who died, sometimes referred to as the *backstory,* 2) the story of how that person died, often called the *event story,* and 3) the story of the feelings, physical responses, and thought patterns that emerged in the early weeks of grief, sometimes referred to as the *impact story.* It is important for mourners to have opportunities to tell these stories.

FINDING A LISTENER

It is not easy to tell these stories, and it is often difficult to find a person who is willing to listen to them. Every culture constructs its own way of dealing with death, having norms that influence practices and practices that shape grieving. In the United States, Canada, and Europe, as well as other countries that might be thought of as "Western," death is largely hidden from view (except for a few grotesque decorations at Halloween), and it is a somewhat taboo subject. George Hagman explains succinctly how this has happened. "With the medicalization of mortality, the removal of the place of death from home to hospital and the responsibility for the disposal of the remains from the family to the professional undertaker, death lost its grounding in the daily lives of Western men and women, eventually becoming invisible." (Hagman, 2016, Chapter 1, p. 13) Keep death out of sight and out of mind is an unspoken cultural norm that inhibits talking about loss.

One can go a short distance into Mexico to find a country with other cultural norms that suggest that death is a part of life, where the deceased are honored in a special way in a holiday called The Day of the Dead, and the extended family often deals with remains and burial, usually including a religious service or even a fiesta of remembrance. Without saying that one culture is better than another, one can at least observe that "telling the story" might be easier in a more receptive culture.

In a culture where death is a taboo subject, speaking as a mourner is often a difficult thing to do. In the well-meaning inquiry of "How are you doing?" there is often body language or a facial expression that suggests: "Please don't tell me." Those who mourn often encounter cliches, platitudes, and formal expressions of sympathy, such as "sorry to hear about your loss," that appear to be designed to discourage further comment. A well-known writer of religious reflections, C.S. Lewis, 1898-1963, shares these observations about avoiding the subject of death in his book, *A Grief Observed,* as cited in Moffat, 1992, p.114)

> An odd by-product of my loss is that I am aware of being
> an embarrassment to everyone I meet. At work, at the club,
> in the street, I see people as they approach me, trying to make
> up their minds whether they'll say something about it or not.

The mourner seldom hears, "Tell me about your loss." What's in the mind of those who don't want to hear about death?

Megan Devine, who herself experienced the sudden loss of her beloved husband, offers some explanations in her helpful book with the catchy title *It's Ok that You're Not Ok.* (Devine, 2017). Many people view grief as a sickness, something to get over, and as quickly as possible, a problem to be solved by the mourner. Stop feeling so bad and put it behind you, is what people are ready to say, when you are still "a howling, shrieking, screaming mass of pain." (Devine, 2017, p. 10) What you really need is "someone to hold your hands while you stand there in blinking horror, staring at the hole that was your life." (Devine, 2017, p. 3) It is not surprising then that "words of intended comfort just grate." (Devine, 2017, p. 14) Mourners may begin to wonder if anyone wants to hear their story. It may be best not to blame individuals for this, knowing that we live in a culture that sends signals to remain silent on this subject. Instead, it may be better to seek out listeners who seem to understand and show an interest in the stories that need to be told, people who want to provide help.

Skilled listeners may be found in professionals who know about grief, are trained as listeners, and are prepared to encourage mourners to tell their stories. A natural listener will also be found sometimes in an untrained but caring friend, neighbor, or colleague. Good listeners are also found in those who have experienced grief, have learned to adjust to it, and have an informed perspective on it. A skilled listener listens but also makes brief responses that show that the one who is struggling to tell the story is being understood. It is especially important to find empathetic listeners for stories involving disenfranchised grief, such as suicide or the loss of a pet.

People can also tell their stories by writing them down, which is a good idea because telling them over and over in one's head is probably a bad idea. Mourners, however, especially need live encounters with caring listeners because telling the story is one of the important tasks of mourning. And it's okay to tell the stories of loss again and again. (Devine, 2017, p. 70)

THE BACKSTORY

Who is the person who died? This question was addressed in detail in Lesson 1. The mediating factors are listed and explained there, but now it is time to describe how they function in a particular loss. If, for example, the person who died was a grandparent or parent, what part did they play in the mourner's life? What were they like? What were their special characteristics? What stands out in remembering them? Or if the person was a spouse or partner, what was the first encounter and how and where did it occur? What was the attraction? How did the initial acquaintance turn into a longer-term relationship? How did the relationship develop and what was it like at the time of death?

The checklists in Lesson 1 are a useful starting point, and it is important to review them, but the challenge now is to provide a narrative description of the individual who has been lost. This can be a story that is written down, or a few notes to be used in telling the story out loud. Selecting and describing the key characteristics and remembered events will help to provide a clear and focused picture. Telling this story is like telling a friend about the main character of a novel or TV drama. What examples and illustrations will convey to the reader or listener a clear description of the one who was lost? Will they glean from this portrait a vivid picture of that person? Perhaps the narrative can close with a brief explanation of the type of relationship it was. Was it a close relationship of high impact or was it ambiguous and confusing? Sketches with broad brushstrokes are best at this point, using the brief checklist in Figure 5 to prepare to tell the backstory.

Figure 5

Checklist for Backstory

_____ kinship or other relationship

_____ physical description

_____ initial encounter or association

_____ personal characteristics

_____ nature and quality of the relationship

_____ remembered examples

_____ illustrations

_____ summary observations

Telling the backstory is important for the listener to gain background information on the person who died. But the more important value of telling the backstory is for the mourner to gain perspective and summarize the essence of the relationship now that the person is gone. A loss has occurred, and the mourner is asking: Who was this person and what was our relationship? How are they remembered? These questions are probably being asked in a new way now.

Dialogue

Mourner: Having had so many losses, I have a lot of stories. I hardly know where to begin.

Counselor: Which are the most difficult to tell?

Mourner: Without passing over the many positive feelings I have about parents, siblings, and my daughter, I would say my spouses are the most difficult to speak of, maybe because of the closeness of those relationships. So, let's begin with my first wife.

Counselor: When did you meet her and how old were you?

Mourner: We met in the college library. We must have both been eighteen. Mere kids. She was very attractive, and I just sat down across from her one evening and started whispering because that's what you did in a library in those days. She was petite and had beautiful reddish-brown hair and warm brown eyes. Smart, too, certainly a better student than I, a music major and pianist. We quickly discovered our common interests in music, art, and the study of religion.

Counselor: Almost destined to be close.

Mourner: Especially in what we valued. We "courted" for four years at an academically challenging college, both of us from working-class families with limited resources beyond our scholarships to cover tuition. So, the highlight of our week was to leave the library on a Friday night—we had Saturday classes—and go to the Student Union and order one milkshake with two straws. We were married the day after graduation.

Counselor: You must have known each other well by that time.

Mourner: Not many people "date" for four years, but we did and grew very close. She shared my interests in religion and so off we went to divinity school, where we lived together in married student housing while I studied, and she worked in the Registrar's Office. A rich aunt sent me what was at the time the huge sum of $3,000, and the summer after my second year, we took half of it and traveled through Italy, France, and Germany using a guidebook called *Europe on Five Dollars a Day.*

Counselor: That must have brought you even closer.

Mourner: Yes, we were enjoying our life together at that time. I concluded that the only way I could decide whether to be a parish minister or not was to try it out, so I became the minister at a small Congregational Church in Ohio. She was perhaps more popular than I at the church—everyone loved her—and the members gave her an elaborate baby shower just before our first child was born.

Counselor: People were drawn to her it seems.

Mourner: And I was proud of that, not jealous. I left that church after two years to work nearby at a historically black college (HBCU). It was during the Civil Rights Movement. That gave me an amazing cross-cultural experience and started my career in higher education administration. Then our second child was born, and as I mentioned earlier, she was blind and physically handicapped. At first, we were drawn closer in trying to figure out how to care for this child, and we seemed to be adjusting. We made it through my doctoral studies as a happy family, but when we arrived in Colorado, we began a demanding therapy program staffed by volunteers to teach our daughter to walk. My conscientious wife was totally devoted to that program and to our young daughter, but that's when I began to feel confused and a little left out. Shortly after that, this beautiful, intelligent, healthy woman was diagnosed with cancer. What was happening to our life?

Counselor: But up to this point, your relationship involved strong attachment, you were calm and happy, and you had built a solid marriage. Let's continue this story later. Who was the other spouse?

Mourner: Fast forward some thirteen years after my first wife's death, passing over that rebound marriage I mentioned earlier. After finishing up the divorce, I was feeling a bit lost and unhappy. An invitation came to me to lead a workshop on college teaching for university faculty in Brazil, and there seated before me and volunteering eagerly for the activities, was this attractive participant, herself a part-time university teacher. She was also petite, a tan-skinned, raven-haired Brazilian beauty with a smashing smile. By that time, I was around fifty-five and she was thirteen years younger at forty-two. Talk about love at first sight!

Counselor: But how did you get to know her?

Mourner: Very thoroughly, through a year-long courtship of letters, weekly phone conversations, and visits back and forth. She came to the US, and I showed her the mountain resorts in Colorado; then she took me to the historic towns and the beaches in Brazil. In the letters we discussed everything: child-raising, religion, politics, values, and it was through those letters that our close attachment grew.

Counselor: Despite being so many miles apart.

Mourner: What surprised me when I reread those letters recently was how cautious I was about entering this new relationship, worried about everything.

Counselor: Maybe rebounding from your rebound marriage.

Mourner: Well put! Yes, I didn't want to make another mistake. But eventually

I invited her to the US on an Alien Fiancé Visa, and we were married. Over that thirty-year relationship, we became two deeply intertwined selves who shared everything, including the joy of raising her delightful daughter. After she finished her master's degree at the university where she had taught in Brazil, she ventured into a new career as a professional translator and Portuguese teacher at several local colleges in Colorado. Together, we redecorated the house, sharing good taste, and made it our home. We took several trips to Europe and Asia, owned time-shares in Mexico, and spent every Friday night together at the local movie theater.

Counselor: It sounds like the old cliché of two hearts becoming one. Close attachments make for painful grief.

Mourner: Yes, you get it, and you can foresee what was to happen. Looking back, rereading those letters, I realize how important happiness was to her from the very beginning, and how happy we were together. That made the loss even more difficult. It was heartbreaking when she died.

THE EVENT STORY

Painful as it may be, telling the event story of how the person died is also important to the mourning process. In Lesson 1, descriptions of various ways that people die are listed and described. It is important to review those lists, but once again the challenge is to provide a narrative description of this particular person's death. This will surely include some mention of whether this was a sudden or prolonged death and whether it was, for example, from natural causes, an accident, or violence. If relevant, one may also report what is known about the physical condition or mental capacity of the person who died.

The event story may also include what impact the form of death is likely to have on the bereaved and the mourning process. As a mediating factor, the form of death is likely to have important implications for mourning, so the focus of this story is on how the manner of death is influencing grief. Telling the event story makes the death more real and harder to deny. Some things to consider for inclusion are listed in Figure 6.

Both the Backstory and the Event Story can be written out or improvised from notes and then shared with an identified listener. If the mourner is in a grief group, stories may also be shared with other members of the group to great advantage to all. Sometimes hearing the story of another mourner can be very illuminating, providing insights and perspectives that might otherwise be missed. Stories of loss are to be told, but also heard. They are often essential to learning from loss.

FIGURE 6

CHECKLIST FOR EVENT STORY

______ manner of death

______ duration of illness or suddenness

______ amount and length of suffering

______ physical condition before death

______ implied mental condition

______ presence or absence of support

______ memories and unknowns

______ regrets

______ implications

DIALOGUE

Counselor: How did your first wife die?

Mourner: I've been revisiting that recently. Although she died from cancer at age forty-two, she was diagnosed five years prior to that.

Counselor: That would be at the young age of thirty-seven.

Mourner: Yes. But she was doing well. The chemotherapy was working. She continued teaching fitness and yoga classes and caring for our children.

Counselor: So, you hadn't expected her to die.

Mourner: That's true. The treatments were over, and she was functioning as if in remission. She was overjoyed at the news from her recent medical appointment, but a month later she began to feel serious pain in her left shoulder blade. They readministered tests and found that the lymphoma had spread. She had only a few months to live. As it turned out, she had only a few weeks to live.

Counselor: So, after thinking she had won the battle with cancer, suddenly she died.

Mourner: I hadn't thought of it that way, but, yes, it was sudden. After believing she was cured, all of us were unprepared for what happened. I regret now that she wasn't in the hospital, but she wanted to be at home. Pain medication reduced her suffering. She went to bed one night, got up a few hours later to visit the bathroom, came back to bed, and as she stretched out, became unconscious, or so we thought. The ambulance personnel tried to revive her, but in a few minutes, they were taking her to the hospital to be pronounced dead.

Counselor: You didn't know what had happened?

Mourner: At the time, no. We only found out later. I went to the hospital with my oldest daughter, a painful experience for her, leaving the disabled daughter with her grandmother, who was in the basement guestroom. But grandma was in such shock, worrying about her daughter, that she never communicated with the blind granddaughter left behind, who then became terribly confused and traumatized, being left alone and uninformed about what had happened to her mother.

Counselor: Perhaps the shock of this death, so sudden for you, contributed to that sense of panic that you described earlier.

Mourner: Oh, yes. I remember that panic setting in soon. The death had been expected as a possibility, but not so soon or traumatic. What we had been expecting for five years was that she would get well. When we got home from the hospital that night, I tried to explain to my two daughters what had happened, and as the reality of our loss began to sink in, I felt that panic creeping over me. How was I going to handle my new responsibilities as a single parent all alone?

Counselor: Later in life, your wife from Brazil died. What were those circumstances?

Mourner: She had an inherited family heart condition, but even on her fifth pacemaker, she was in good health. She had survived a stroke ten years earlier, losing both languages, but coming back strong with speech therapy and a lot of hard work. Eventually her failing heart led to accumulation of fluid in her abdomen, but it was drained every two weeks for more than a year, and she was doing fine.

Counselor: Another situation with serious illness, but apparent good health.

Mourner: Yes, similar in that respect. Taking good care of her was the natural thing for me to do, and I never thought much about her dying because she was doing so well. Her quiet, persistent, and cheerful demeanor gave no clue that her death was not far away.

Counselor: Her good cheer and quiet hope put away your fears.

Mourner: Perhaps to the point that I may have developed some denial. Then one day her daughter was with me visiting her in the hospital, and the doctors told us that they couldn't do any more for her and that we should consider home hospice. We both struggled to hold back our tears. That meant she was dying.

Counselor: The news was a surprise, but not really surprising.

Mourner: The turning point was that she had lost a considerable amount of short-term memory and had become disoriented. Her daughter and I made arrangements for a hospital bed in a room at home—the same house where my first wife had died—and her kind, loving daughter and I, along with visiting hospice workers, took care of her for six months. She received her bowl of fruit each morning, but when she was asked what she had for breakfast, she couldn't remember. In fact, she couldn't even remember whether she had had breakfast.

Counselor: You both experienced her gradual decline.

Mourner: Yes, we knew where this was going but we didn't know when or how it would end. On the one hand, we had already lost much of the person we had known, and yet the essential characteristics of her personality were still intact: her strong faith, her hope for the future, her calm attitude. When asked how she was, she always replied, "I'm doing fine." Above all, her unforgettable smile captivated all the hospice workers caring for her.

Counselor: Were you able to talk to her about what was happening to her?

Mourner: I never knew whether I could do that because I never tried. I didn't know how to ask. It is one of my regrets.

Counselor: You didn't want to disturb her peaceful equilibrium?

Mourner: Exactly. We didn't need a conversation about dying that ended with both of us crying. So, we continued the hospice at home until it was no longer safe to get her out of bed. She went to an assisted living facility and died there after eighteen days. My other regret is that I wasn't with her when she died.

Counselor: Was that important to her?

Mourner: I'm not sure it was. I'm guessing that she felt she was already in God's hands.

The Impact Story

The mourner's third story is probably the most difficult to tell. It includes the greater challenge of identifying and sharing the feelings of loss that surfaced during the early weeks of grief. This story may include not only a host of difficult feelings, but certain physical responses to grief and the often-confusing thoughts that may accompany loss. This is also a story that can be written out but is more likely to be told aloud in pieces to a counselor one-on-one, to a grief educator and grief group members, to healthcare professionals in shorter segments, or to clergy during visits. This is the impact story of the loss.

Before we examine in greater depth the difficult feelings associated with loss, we need to step back and gain perspective by asking: Where do these feelings come from and why is so much disorientation experienced by those who grieve? In recent years, rapid progress has been made through the emerging field of neuroscience in describing certain functions of the brain and their location in different parts of the brain. Some of this science of the brain is now being applied to what happens when there is significant disruption through loss. What happens in the brain when there is grief? Mary-Frances O'Connor reports some of this neuroscience in her recent book, *The Grieving Brain*. There is growing evidence that the brain is working on our behalf in many ways without our having to instruct it to do so. But it's not always what we expect or want.

The brain makes virtual maps, the equivalent of big-picture maps of our surroundings so that we know where things are and how to get around. It makes reliable predictions of actions, such as a spouse returning home at six o'clock each day as expected. What happens to the brain when death occurs? O'Connor compares it to waking up in the middle of the night and finding the dining room table gone. It is missing and is unexplainably not there. It should be there, but it isn't. This is very difficult to understand. The brain has serious problems with that. It knows that the table has been there and how it has been used. The mental map says that it should be there. Likewise with loss, the mental map doesn't work anymore. O'Connor explains how this functions with grief. (O'Connor, 2022, pp. 3-14)

The table may be there, but one less place setting is needed. The person who is supposed to be there is gone. They no longer exist. "The idea that a person simply does not exist anymore does not follow the rules the brain has learned over a lifetime." (O'Connor, 2022, p.14) And so, the brain must adjust to this disturbing information, and it takes time. One way to look at this explanation is to interpret grief as something that happens *to* us, actually *to* all of us, and that the disorientation that comes with loss is not just ours alone, but a universal response because we all have brains that want to know what happened. Grief is our vigilant brain looking out for us when reliable mental maps have been disrupted.

The brain's search for understanding, however, is our search, and the words used to describe the experience, such as *shattering* or *disruptive* still apply. It helps to understand what is going on in the brain, but the feelings will explode anyway. We are left to process the pain as the brain tries to figure out what happened.

As we will learn in Lesson 3, grief is addressed over time and has associated with it certain tasks. One of these tasks, as outlined by J. William Worden is to "Process the Pain of Grief." (Worden, 2018, p.45ff) In the remainder of this lesson, we focus on identifying and expressing that pain in the Impact Story. Worden has compiled a comprehensive list of feelings, physical responses, and thought patterns associated with normal grief. (Worden, 2018, pp.20-31) We have drawn extensively on Worden's illuminating work here, rearranged the order, and developed short summaries of these foundational concepts. In a few instances we have deleted or added ideas, along with inserting typical "I" statements that summarize feelings.

What follows is a list of things to look for, whether as mourner or helper. Of course, not everyone will experience all of these reactions to loss, but most will experience some of them. It is important to be aware of and recognize them as natural and normal in the process of grieving. As Megan DeVine reminds us, not only in the title but in the substance of her book, "it's okay that you're not okay." (DeVine, 2017) That's what grief involves, feeling unusually upset, sad, and maybe even speechless at first, or perhaps not in control of one's outward expression of emotion. As the playwright Seneca, 4 BCE-65 CE, wrote in *Hippolytus,* Act II, Scene 3, as cited in Moffat, 1992, p.21.

Light griefs can speak;
great ones are dumb.

Typical Feelings

Numbness. Sometimes the first feeling is the sensation of no feeling at all. This may come with the initial shock of notification or awareness of the loss. Numbness may serve as a protection from being overwhelmed with feelings. *I just can't feel anything.*

Shock. Often associated with an unexpected death, shock can also arise with anticipated death as a sudden awakening to an awareness of what has happened. *I can't believe this is really happening.*

Sadness. A general feeling of sadness sometimes hangs like a cloud over everything and brings the sensation of needing to cry. *I'm so sad, I just want to cry all the time.*

Anger. Out of frustration that nothing could be done or was done, feelings of anger can arise. Even with inevitable death, there is often anger at being left alone, anger that there was so much suffering, or anger that the universe is designed with death for every living creature. *I'm infuriated.*

Blame. With anger sometimes comes blame, making someone responsible for this death, with the idea that it could have been prevented. *I want to get to the bottom of this.*

Guilt. When blame turns inward, it becomes self-blaming, sometimes producing shame or guilt. What did I neglect? How could I have let this happen? Why didn't I do something? When these become the dominant questions, they are often an expression of feelings of guilt. *I could have done better.*

Helplessness. Loss of hope can lead to a feeling of not knowing what to do next, a belief that nothing can be done, or a general sense of helplessness. No one seems to be appearing to offer help. *I don't know how I'm going to survive.*

Anxiety. With so many uncertain and unresolved things appearing on the horizon, anxiety can result. Internalized confusion can cause generalized worry. *I'm getting really nervous.*

Loneliness. Not everyone is left completely alone, but some are. Even when others are around, loneliness for the deceased may be pervasive and painful. *I'm suddenly out in the middle of nowhere.*

Fatigue and hyperactivity. When an active life is interrupted by death, daily routines may be disrupted and rendered pointless. A sense of apathy may set in and lead to feelings of fatigue without apparent reason. However, some who experience loss may engage in unusual hyperactivity. Running around all day can lead to genuine fatigue at night. *I'm feeling exhausted.*

Relief. Sometimes grief is experienced as relief. This may be the relief that comes when suffering has ended, or it may be the hard-to-express relief coming from extensive caretaking or the end of a stressful relationship. *At least it's over.*

Typical Physical Responses

Sleep Disturbance. After a loss, going to sleep may be difficult and going back to sleep after awakening in the middle of the night may be even more difficult. The mind keeps finding things to think about and worry over. In most cases the disorder corrects itself with time or mourners learn to control it. *I'm losing so much sleep.*

Dreams. Dreams can be "sweet" or disturbing. Dreams can be nightmares of trauma associated with the manner of death. Pleasant memories can also be shaped into dreams. Sometimes they can be disturbing because they involve realistic appearances of the deceased. *I'm having strange dreams.*

Eating Disorders. Sometimes people who are seldom sick get digestive upset associated with grief. The tendency is to eat too little through loss of appetite. *I've lost interest in food.*

Crying and Sobbing. Extended and spontaneous crying set off by an unexpected remembrance will be common, sometimes including deep and nearly uncontrollable sobbing. Crying is normal and necessary, and learning to control where it happens and how long it lasts can be a challenge. Crying is sometimes replaced with sighing, drawing in, holding, and releasing deep breaths. *I can't seem to stop crying.*

THOUGHT PATTERNS

Disbelief. Not believing that it has really happened is a common reaction to loss. Coming to terms with the reality of death is important and getting the mind to face it honestly is a first step. *I can't believe this is happening.*

Distraction. Forgetting recent actions, getting confused, or losing purpose and direction are common responses of the bereaved. Those are common responses of older people, too, and may be aggravated by loss, making for more confusion than usual. *I seem so lost and confused.*

Obsessive Thoughts. Thinking the same words or phrases over and over again is a common reaction of those who grieve. Sometimes the thoughts are about the deceased; at other times they seem random or even nonsensical. Designed to reduce anxiety, obsessions sometimes make things worse. *I can't get it out of my head.*

Hallucinations. During the early weeks of grief, visual and auditory hallucinations may occur, such as hearing or seeing the deceased when it may be something or someone else entirely. Although these may be normal for a while, vivid hallucinations, especially those related to a traumatic death, may be troublesome and persistent. Hallucinations may be comforting to some at first, but help may be needed to get them to go away. *I see or hear things that make me wonder if I am losing my mind.*

Preparing to Tell the Impact Story

Having reviewed the lists of typical feelings, physical responses, and thought patterns, one may begin to ask which of these apply to a particular mourner. Some people will experience nearly everything on these lists; others will not. Some will experience them frequently; others occasionally or not at all. For some the experience will be intense, for others, not so strong. Think of these as words that can be crafted into sentences that will tell the unique story of a mourner who has experienced the pain of an incomparable and distinctive loss. What has been the impact of this loss? A personal profile of loss can be developed by responding to the Checklist of Feelings presented in Figure 7. This profile becomes the foundation for the impact story to be told.

FIGURE 7

CHECKLIST OF FEELINGS

Check the items that have been experienced and skip over those that have not, noting degrees of frequency and intensity for those experienced.

	Frequency			Intensity		
	High	Moderate	Low	High	Moderate	Low
Numbness						
Shock						
Sadness						
Anger						
Blame						
Guilt						
Helplessness						
Anxiety						
Loneliness						
Fatigue						
Relief						
Sleeplessness						
Dreams						

	Frequency			Intensity		
	High	Moderate	Low	High	Moderate	Low
Eating						
Crying						
Disbelief						
Distraction						
Obsession						
Hallucinations						

The challenge now is to move beyond this somewhat formal analysis to the words, expressions, descriptions, details and illustrations needed to tell an individual's unique story of personal loss. At some point this impact story needs to be told, either by writing it down or expressing it to sympathetic listeners. As we will describe in Lesson 3, processing the pain is one of several tasks in dealing with grief, but as Worden points out, the goal is not "recovery" but "adaptation." (Worden, 2018, p. 7) Most people are resilient and will adapt (Bonanno, 2019, Chapter 4), but the process is painful and can go on for a long time. How long?

The author Mark Twain, 1835–1913, born as Samuel Clemens, is best known for his adventure stories of Tom Sawyer and Huckleberry Finn, but he also wrote this in an *Autobiography,* as cited in Moffat, 1992 p.6.

The mind has a dim sense of vast loss—that is all.
It will take mind and memory months and possibly
years to gather the details and thus learn and know
the whole extent of the loss.

Twain's intuitions of more than a century ago seem to coincide with modern neuroscience. The brain needs a lot of time to figure out what happened. What has also been documented is that human contact can help, underscoring the need for listeners to the stories of loss. The intensity of grief often sets off panic, but panic motivates people to come into contact with other people. When that happens, neuroscience explains, positive chemicals, the equivalent of opiates, are generated, and these function to soothe and reduce stress. Apparently, the tumult of emotions and feelings related to loss can be reduced through meaningful human contact. Wouldn't it be nice, Mary-Frances O'Connor suggests, to find a doctor who recommends, "To temporarily relieve your distress, have two conversations with caring people, preferably including a hug, and call me in the morning." (O'Connor, 2022, p 167)

DIALOGUE

Counselor: Can you tell me about the period of mourning when your first wife died?

Mourner: Some rather traditional things happened. A well-off wife of a professional football player, a friend of my wife's brother, took it upon herself to prepare a lovely and elaborate memorial reception at the university. My older daughter and I just needed to appear; all the planning was done by the kind friend. Many people attended, mostly adult students from my wife's yoga and fitness classes. Over the years, she attracted many followers who came again and again to those classes, which had an ambiance of spirituality about them; and she had become their admired leader, radiating a certain calm through her voice and movement. Naturally, some of my colleagues attended as well, many of whom had taken her classes. My daughter and I remember some very sad cello music being played, but we were awed by her mother's following. In some ways, we felt like observers.

Counselor: So, a somewhat formal and sizable public reception was held as a memorial.

Mourner:Yes, followed by a more spiritual service at our family church where my daughter's school friends, neighbors, and relatives supported us through a more intimate remembrance with readings and traditional church music. There was a much smaller and sadder family service at the funeral home, with the embalmed body resting in an open casket.

Counselor: Three very diverse opportunities for memorializing your wife then.

Mourner: Yes, as it was done in those days, but a bit of a blur to me today. And when they were over, and her body had been sent back to Ohio to be buried next to her father, the traditional mourning had been completed. Who was I to know that something more was needed for expressing my grief?

Counselor: And you were panicked about your responsibilities. So, in some ways traditional mourning led you to bypass the process of dealing more directly with your feelings.

Mourner: Yes, and for my children as well. Oh, I'm sure there was shock and sadness, but mostly anxiety about an uncertain future and a sense of helplessness underlying my panic. I had no physical responses or troublesome thought patterns, and I hardly remember crying and sobbing. I don't remember telling much of this to anyone. But I do remember jumping into action, facing an overload of parenting and household tasks.

Counselor: The dominant message in your mind was "get on with it."

Mourner: Yes, and don't waste time with sad feelings. Looking back after many years, I feel a sense of shame that I did so little to acknowledge this loss, to deal with mixed feelings, or any feelings. I remember going to a psychiatrist to explore some of those feelings and his response was "some things go unresolved."

Counselor: And indeed, they did.

Mourner: I felt the world peering over my shoulder to make sure I was holding up and being strong.

Counselor: So, your own loss and grief became transformed into a need to replace this loss with action—and soon.

Mourner: I know that failing to grieve had its consequences for me and my daughters. The younger one never quite got over being left alone the night her mother died. As my older daughter went off to college, she found her friends having their moms to help them with the first year transition, and when they talked about their moms, she knew hers was gone. It made her feel a little distant from her peers, even though she still had me as her dad. My guilt at not mourning lingers around the word "disrespectful," simply not honoring with appropriate frequency and intensity the feelings I must have been having and rushing into a rebound marriage which must have been hard on my immediate and extended family.

Counselor: And as you were left to parenting on your own, you probably felt a need to be emotionally strong for your two children.

Mourner: Yes, I believe this perceived imperative to be strong ruled out a lot of normal sadness and crying.

Counselor: So, you were rebounding from the loss and bypassing the feelings of loss as well, and now you regret that, though you understand it.

Mourner: Very much so. Sometimes I feel like I've been going through life carrying a suitcase of regrets about the lack of mourning for her, feeling guilty for having that baggage, but ashamed when I try to set it aside.

Counselor: Most people carry some sort of unwanted baggage from their past. Acknowledging it may help to minimize its weight. But eventually, you've told me, you found a way to build a happy and productive life with another spouse.

Mourner: And there was certainly no lack of mourning filled with deep feeling when that loss occurred.

Counselor: So, tell me about the recent loss of your Brazilian wife. Was that a different story? If so, in what ways?

Mourner: I was much older and had experienced many more losses by that time, including my handicapped daughter's death from ovarian cancer. Even though I had cared for my wife at home for six months, I felt shocked in coping with the reality of her death. I would never see her again, never see that smile, or hear her voice say, "I'm doing fine." Really. I felt an intense sadness at her loss, not just as "my loss," but at her being gone, without life and the existence she cherished so much.

Counselor: Confronting the finality and reality of her death must have been difficult for you at that stage of life, being retired and so interdependent on each other.

Mourner: Yes. I certainly had no one to be angry with about her death; everyone did their best, including the medical staff and her loving daughter. But I do remember a kind of existential anger about all life, including human life, ending in death. Why was the universe set up like that? I guess that I was outraged that such a wonderful person had to die.

Counselor: And you weren't sure who to blame for that?

Mourner: I had no one to blame and no self-blaming or personal guilt about her death. We had a beautiful relationship, and I had cared for her to the best of my ability, but now it was over, and I wasn't sure what I would do with my life, living alone in that same house with reminders of her everywhere I turned.

Counselor: Without her, naturally you began to feel lonely?

Mourner: Yes, and sad. Gloom was everywhere around me. I cried a lot and sobbed deeply, repeatedly. The slightest thing would set it off—a travel souvenir, a song, a memory of something we had done together. It seemed as if I was sobbing continually, hour after hour, day after day.

Counselor: Not sure it would ever end, I suppose.

Mourner: Then I began to think of my own death. Remember, I was older than she, and I began to wonder how I would die. Those obsessive thoughts came up frequently during the day, sometimes even first thing in the morning as I woke to another day. I would remind myself to stop worrying because I was in good health, but then I remembered that in my experience that's who dies, the healthy ones.

Counselor: That death can come out of nowhere. But how did you deal with those feelings?

Mourner: Lucky for me, I didn't have any physical consequences or too many disturbing thought patterns. Well, maybe just a couple. In the spring, strong winds set in motion a light-weight outdoor rocker, and to me it looked like she was sitting there rocking. When the house creaked in those winds, I thought I heard her out in the kitchen preparing breakfast.

Counselor: An imagined presence, but not actual disturbing images.

Mourner: Correct. Mostly it was just my intense loneliness and sadness I had to deal with. Her daughter was going through some of this as well, missing her mom, and we stayed in touch. I held a Remembrance Day for my wife. Naturally her daughter attended, and my daughter came down from Canada, and a surprising number of former work colleagues came to that to support me.

Looking back now, I can see how I reconnected that day with many people who I later came to socialize with in the weeks and months after that. I was moved by and accepted their invitations to lunch or dinner, which became a kind of springboard into a new life for me. I learned to talk about her to those people without sobbing.

Counselor: Beginning to get control, at least. Then what?

Mourner: I went on with those feelings of sadness and loneliness for several weeks, but eventually I was invited to attend a five-week grief education workshop associated with the hospice care provider. It was there that I began to hear the stories of other mourners and learn about their loss. I discovered that there are some things that you can do to deal with it.

Counselor. Yes, there are resources. Let me hand you this list of things to try. Ways to adapt.

Mourner: Okay. I'll take a look at it. There is so much to learn from loss.

References

Bonanno, G.A. (2019). *The Other Side of Sadness:What the New Science of Bereavement Tells about Life After Loss.* New York: Basic Books.

DeVine, M. (2017). *It's OK That You're Not OK.* Boulder, CO: Sounds True.

Hagman, G. (Ed.) (2016). *New Models of Bereavement, Theory and Treatment.* New York: Routledge.

Moffat, M.J. (1992). *In the Midst of Winter: Selections from the Literature of Mourning.* New York; Random House.

O'Connor, M-F. (2022). *The Grieving Brain.* New York: Harper Collins Publishers.

Worden, J.W. (2018). *Grief Counseling and Grief Therapy: A Handbook for Mental Health Practitioners,* Fifth Edition. New York: Springer Publishing.

LESSON 3

LEARNING TO COPE WITH LOSS AND TRYING THINGS THAT MIGHT HELP

DEFINING AND DESCRIBING GRIEF

What is grief and what form does it take? It is a response to a serious loss through the death of someone close, but what does it involve? How has its definition changed over time? Can mourners be helped?

STAGES

At one time, grief was thought of as taking place in stages. In 1969, a medical doctor named Elizabeth Kubler-Ross described the arrival of death in a sequence of stages experienced by the patient who is dying. Her outline of those stages became well known through her book *On Death and Dying*. She and co-author David Kessler adapted those ideas to describe stages of grief in *On Grief and Grieving*. (Kubler-Ross and Kessler, 2005) The concept of stages had a strong influence on how people came to think about the process of grieving.

A stage involves a period of time, and although it may vary in length, one stage follows another, and the assumption is that a stage is completed before moving on to the next. The stages are summarized in *Finding Meaning*, a later work by Kessler and quoted as follows:

Denial: shock and disbelief that loss has occurred
Anger: that someone we love is no longer here
Bargaining: all the what-ifs and regrets
Depression: sadness from loss
Acceptance: acknowledging the reality of loss
   —(Kessler, 2019, p. 1)

The Kubler-Ross stages suggest that certain things occur at each stage and must be dealt with, passed through and not skipped over, to arrive at the next stage, eventually finding "closure" as acceptance. At least this is how the stages were interpreted, perhaps giving them more structure and importance than Kubler-Ross had intended. She had a stroke and was disabled for nine years, later in her life writing about the long period of anticipatory grief created for those who know a loved one is dying. At one point she wrote, "I am so much more than five stages. And so are you." (Kubler-Ross and Kessler, 2005, p. 216)

The eventual objection to the five stages was both about the content of the stages and the concept of grief as stages to be addressed in order, one by one, until arriving at closure. Today, those who study grief have set forth other ways to think about the grief process without using the concept of stages.

DETACHMENT

Another description of grief, strongly criticized today, goes back to the writings of Sigmund Freud, a view that shaped and dominated thinking about grief for many decades. Freud's classic idea of grief is that the bereaved must withdraw "emotional energy in the deceased in order to invest it in living relationships." (Hagman, 2016, p. xxv) The idea is found in Freud's writing in *Totem and Taboo* (1912) where grief's function is described as "to detach the survivor's memories and hopes from the dead." (Shelby cited in Hagman, 2016, p. 67) The technical term for that process is *decathexis,* where *cathexis* is investing emotional energy in a person, the *de* part being to take that investment away because the person is dead. Decathexis might more simply be described as "letting go." (Hagman, 2016, p. 7) Freud's ideas became the standard model for thinking about grief and the concept of detachment became nearly universal. (Hagman, 2016, p.1)

Becoming detached from one's loss is not easy, however, and was described as work. The term "grief work" was originally used by the psychiatrist Erich Lindeman in 1944 "to describe the tasks and processes" to "resolve grief," suggesting that bereaved persons need to get over their malaise by becoming actively involved in the process of detachment. (Rando, 1991, p. 16) Becoming actively involved is still valued, but the so-called "work" of grief is now described differently.

Knowing these bits of history is important for understanding newer ideas that are replacing them, but also to notice how older concepts are still affecting general cultural attitudes about grief. The idea that grief is a sickness that one must get over, stop talking about, and move on from as soon as possible, is still with us as a cultural norm. As Megan DeVine points out "grief is not a problem to be solved." It's not a disorder. There's not something wrong with you. You're not stuck in a stage. You don't have to stop being so sad. (DeVine, 217, pp. 15, 26, 27) The older Freudian idea of detachment from the person who died lives on. Deeply embedded ideas don't just fade away.

GRIEF AS TASKS

Although many new ideas about grief are still being developed and expressed, perhaps the simplest and most useful concept is *tasks*. A person who is grieving has certain things to do. Completing these tasks does not assure the end of pain nor even a better life, but looking at grief as tasks instead of stages or detachment provides a useful way of organizing a response. Tasks don't have to be done in order, skipping one to get to another is not a problem, nor is there a time limit. Doing them all with a degree of success does not necessarily result in closure.

Those who have described human development at various points in life, such as Erik Erikson and Robert Havinghurst, often use the phrase "developmental tasks," meaning the things that people work on at different points in life. Tasks are things to do, and when developmental psychologists watch people at a particular age, they notice that they tend to be working on characteristic tasks for that age group. The same method can be used in the study of grief: observe people who are grieving and notice which tasks they are working on, then summarize them and describe them to create a better understanding of grief.

For those who are grieving, a very useful and well-elaborated list of tasks can be found in J. William Worden's *Grief Counseling and Grief Therapy*, Fifth Edition. We paraphrase and summarize Worden's four tasks of grieving here, giving him full credit for these ideas. (Worden, 2018, Chapter 2, pp. 39-58) Choosing the order for working on the tasks and the time spent on each is left to the preferences of those who are grieving, but these are tasks that most will face sooner or later in varying degrees of difficulty. They all require effort and involvement and might be thought of as guidelines for a new kind of grief work, one that comes with neither the requirement of completion nor guarantees of satisfaction.

ACCEPTING THE REALITY OF THE LOSS

Mary Jane Moffat in *Widow's Supper* as cited in Moffat, 1992, p. 132.

Through the blowing curtain
the late sun presents
movement and shade
to the cloth, the cutlery,
the single plate.

Facing the reality of the person's death is a key task. Not facing it is characterized as *denial*, ranging from minor confusion of the deceased with people seen on the street to strong mental delusions of the person's presence. Sometimes people maintain an extra dinner place-setting (instead of the single plate) or maintain undisturbed, the arrangements of an entire room ready for the return of the deceased. Feelings of loss can also be denied by saying things like "I know they are still here." Well-intended spiritual beliefs sometimes serve as assurances of an imminent reunion, while seances can provide supposedly live conversations with the deceased. Beliefs in being reunited sometimes get in the way of arriving at an honest sense of acceptance of the loss. The intellectual and emotional task of acceptance takes time depending on the manner of death, but the task is important and involves accepting that the loss is real, and that the death has actually occurred.

Processing the Pain of Grief

Maimonides, 1135–1204, in *Guide to the Perplexed* as cited in Moffat, 1992, p. 100.

> Those who grieve find comforts in weeping and arousing their sorrow until the body is too tired to bear the inner emotions.

Grief hurts emotionally and sometimes physically. It can also be extremely tiring when it is unrelieved. Processing the pain is the task, as opposed to avoiding or suppressing it or just enduring it. The way people experience the pain of grief varies. Some may describe it as a chronic sense of sadness or emptiness. Others emphasize the wave-like experience of being suddenly consumed by a force that erupts uncontrollably within, challenging the capacity to stay collected and composed. Whichever way it occurs, the pain must be processed as suggested in Lesson 2, by telling the story of the loss. This allows for the expression of pain and associated thoughts, memories, and reactions, by sharing it with listeners who may be able to provide empathy and insight as the story unfolds.

While most people need to tell their story aloud to others, some with more introverted personalities may prefer to write it out or process it internally in solitude. Expressing pain is not easy, but avoidance can become problematic. The path toward denial can even lead to an actual loss of feeling, cutting off feelings rather than processing them. The pain of grief can also be soothed through drugs and alcohol or the quick cure of intense travel, fleeing the place, the person, and the feelings. The task is not to avoid, soothe, or escape the feelings, but to face them, to identify them, and process them by talking or writing about them. Dealing with the pain at the time of the loss is better than carrying it on through life.

Adjusting to a World without the Deceased

Paiute Indian Song in *Lament of a Man for His Son* as cited in Moffat, 1992, p.59.

What is my life to me, now you are departed?

The process of adjustment to a world without the deceased will vary depending on mediating factors, such as the kinship relationship, the various roles played by the deceased, and the degree of change being caused by the loss. External changes can include taking on new roles and responsibilities and building new skills. This task can also include internal challenges of redefining oneself. The question becomes, who am I now? When loss occurs, one's perception of the world is changed. Strong attachments when broken by loss can affect one's sense of adequacy and capability, self-efficacy, and self-esteem. The task is to face the new world brought on by loss and rebuild one's life through appropriate external and internal changes. (Lesson 4.) This task may also include dealing with the disruption of a sense of meaning and a new search for how to make sense out of life. (Lesson 5)

Remembering the Deceased and Going on with Life

Robert Frost, 1874–1963, in *Home Burial,* cited in Moffat, 1992, p.65.

The little graveyard where my people are!
So small the window frames the whole of it.
Not so much larger than a bedroom, is it.

Remembering the deceased may begin with a small graveyard, but the idea of memorializing is much broader than a cemetery marker. Quite the opposite of Freud's concept of withdrawing emotional energy, memorializing means finding meaningful ways to continue the memory of the deceased with new and creative connections, sometimes referred to as *continuing bonds*. Instead of turning away from the deceased, the task is to find new ways of extending that relationship and incorporating it into the rest of life's journey. It involves going on with life and remembering the deceased in one's new day-to-day activity and emotional life in a natural and positive way.

Grief and Time

Although the idea of tasks has replaced the concept of stages, the intensity of pain and severity of suffering still appear to be related in some way to the passage of time. Although a person may continue to deal with aspects of grief a year or more after the loss, what happens in the first few weeks is generally described as much more intense by those who grieve.

A more recent model of grieving speaks to the passage of time by establishing periods called Early Grief, Middle Grief, and Later Grief, while characterizing the responses as Reacting, Reconstructing, and Reorienting. (Neimeyer, 2016, pp. 5-11) The tasks that the mourner chooses to focus on as well as the activities selected for coping with grief may vary considerably depending on how far or close the mourner is from the actual date when the loss occurred. How quickly the mourner adapts to grief over periods of time, however, varies considerably. As Gary Roe states, "Grief has its own timetable." For some it is a sprint, for others, a marathon. (Roe, 2015, pp. 33-34)

So, if grief begins at the moment of loss, how long does it last? Mourners want to know how long their grief will continue. Naturally, the answer is "it depends." The description of tasks reveals that grief is not one thing but a combination of different tasks. Some of the tasks may be addressed more quickly, such as accepting the reality of the loss; others will take more time, such as adjusting to a world without the deceased. We have already explored in Lesson 2 the task of processing the pain through telling the stories. Adjusting to a changed world and remembering the deceased are explored in Lesson 4. It appears that people can adapt to certain aspects of grief in a reasonably short period of time. For others, it takes much longer. But there seems to be a consensus among those who grieve that some aspects of grieving never go away completely. Vivid memories, strong feelings, and persistent behaviors continue in the background or pop up at predictable times of the year at special events or holidays. As some mourners insist, every day is Memorial Day. The poet Percy Bysshe Shelly, 1792-1822, concludes *Adonis* with these words, as cited in Moffat, 1992, p.99.

> Ah woe is me! Winter is come and gone,
> But grief returns with the revolving year.

RESILIENCE

The tasks outlined by Worden are the things that mourners seem to address in periods of grief over time. They spend more effort with some tasks than others, not taking them in any particular order, perhaps being more successful with some and less diligent with others. But in general, most people who work through the tasks of grieving can go on living life without serious problems that need treatment. They may get help of some sort, often informally, as they address the tasks of grief, but they usually get better without formal therapy. Such people are referred to as resilient.

Resilience is a major theme in the book by George A. Bonanno called *The Other Side of Sadness: What the New Science of Bereavement Tells about Life after Loss*. In setting forth a new model of bereavement, Bonanno points out that grief tends to come not in stages, but in waves, that many people are sad one moment, but laughing in another, a condition called *oscillation*. He suggests "that grief is tolerable because it comes and goes." (Bonanno, 2019, pp. 59-61)

Studies of resilience suggest that formal grief counseling may have been overprescribed in the past. Bonanno asserts "most bereaved people don't need treatment" and may not be helped by it. (Bonanno, 2018, p. 157) Although this may make sense when referring to "formal" treatment, resilience doesn't preclude the need for less formal "help" as those who grieve try to address their tasks. The process of becoming resilient can still be very painful and confusing. Having a trained psychotherapist may not be essential, but having a skilled helper at one's side, such as a counselor, social worker, or member of the clergy, to provide understanding and encouragement is often beneficial. A helper who listens well and cares about the bereaved can ease the pain of loss, particularly in the early period of grief.

Complicated Grief

Bonanno states that only 10-15% of people have grief reactions that interfere with their life. (Bonanno, 2019, p.140) For that small percentage, grief takes over, and they may feel lost, aimless, and hopeless. For complicated grief, where people become dysfunctional because grief runs too deep and too long, some grief therapy may be necessary. (Bonanno, 2018, pp.140-141) The official term is Prolonged Complicated Bereavement Disorder (PCBD). It is sometimes called *chronic grief, delayed grief, pathological grief,* or *unresolved grief.* (Worden, 2018, pp. 3, 137) Complicated grief is a type of grief that has a higher intensity and longer duration, but its most distinguishing characteristic is that it interferes in one or more ways with living a "normal" life. It is usually associated with mediating factors that make natural resilience difficult. Adaptation to grief becomes more challenging because something else is often taking place at the same time.

What are the factors that can complicate the grief process? The manner of death, including the degree of shock or violence, can have an influence. Highly ambivalent or dependent relationships with the deceased, reactivated psychological wounds, unfulfilled aspirations involving the deceased, or a general sense of helplessness, can all come into play. Grief is also aggravated by the uncertainty associated with an unverified death, by multiple deaths (sometimes called *bereavement overload*), and by a history of previous losses or depressive illness. Personality features, such as a limited capacity to cope with distress and a negative self-concept, along with a weak social support system leading to social isolation can also contribute to prolonged or more intense grief. This ultimately leads to a feeling of being overwhelmed that seems interminable. In essence, complicated grief is when adaptation is not taking place, grief tasks are not being addressed, and sufficient healing and mending is not happening as other factors interrupt the process. Signs of dysfunction may include extended work or school absences, increased use or abuse of substances, or clinical diagnoses of anxiety, depression, phobia, or PTSD. A key element to look for is *maladaptive behavior,* doing things that make the process of adaptation worse instead of better. (Worden, 2018, pp. 131-148)

Bearing in mind that only 10-15% of those who are mourning tend toward complicated grief as opposed to natural resilience, the probability of having complicated grief is low; but if it occurs, it may need to be addressed. Sometimes people need help in determining if they have it. If so, counselors trained in grief therapy can be accessed, and continuing problems can be assessed. People who fit the profile, would likely benefit from professional counseling to resolve their complicated grief.

GRIEF AND COGNITIVE CONTROL

Having learned about resilience and complicated grief, it is natural to want to move in the direction of resilience while avoiding the path to complicated grief. Is there a way to do things that might lead more directly toward resilience? We know that complicated grief often involves other factors that can contribute to it, but there may be some things that can happen in the early weeks of grief that may enhance the quest for resilience.

Although grief initially involves strong feelings and deep emotions, adaptation will not necessarily be achieved just by expressing these feelings to others. Coping with strong feelings includes what the mourner thinks about those feelings. The important contribution of cognitive behavioral therapy (CBT) is the suggestion that negative or distorted thinking habits have a significant impact on our behavior and emotions. While most people engage in some unhelpful thinking tendencies, these may become magnified and problematic for mourners having the intense experience of loss of a loved one. The key to cognitive awareness is realizing that we need not fall victim to the thoughts that enter our mind and seem to shape our emotional experience. Instead, we can learn to identify and challenge dysfunctional or unrealistic thoughts and exchange them for more realistic, helpful ones. Retraining our thought patterns can instigate shifts in related emotions and behaviors and bring about a greater sense of control and well-being, one important step toward resilience.

Ruth Malkinson explains how the basic ideas of cognitive therapy were expanded on and developed into a theory called Rational Emotive Behavioral Therapy (REBT) through the work of Albert Ellis during the 1960s. (Malkinson, 2007, p.80 ff.) This work has become especially helpful in thinking about grief therapy today. Ellis noticed that people engage in a lot of "self-talk," and not all of it is helpful. In fact, depending on what that talk is, it can become disturbing, damaging, and maladaptive. He proposed the ABC model of (A) an activating event, which in grief is loss through death of a loved one, followed by (B) beliefs that grow out of that event, and (C) consequences of the beliefs. Note that consequences come from beliefs about the event, not directly from the event itself.

Beliefs (B) can be of two kinds. Irrational, dysfunctional and maladaptive beliefs, that tend to lean toward self-condemnation and blame, can lead to consequences of depression and anxiety. On the other hand, rational, functional and adaptive beliefs can lead toward normal feelings of sadness and sorrow but also to the more positive consequence of adaptation to those feelings in a positive way.

The problem is that there is a strong human "tendency to think irrationally about the event," especially the irreversible adverse event of death. (Malkinson, 2007, p.86) Mourners start to say things to themselves like: How could they have done this to me? Life is so unfair. I feel guilty for living (survivor's guilt) and completely lost, without purpose or direction. I want to get rid of my haunting memories because they only make me cry. I don't want any sad reminders around. Very often these thoughts and meanings attributed to events have an irrational aspect that can be examined and modified. It is possible (a choice) to have more positive, rational, and realistic interpretations of the loss, more adaptive cognitions, that lead to a better adjustment. This choice one has over interpreting thoughts and feelings is called "inner control." (Malkinson, 2007, p. 107, 116)

The typical forms of negative self-talk have been elaborated for counselors and popularized for a general audience in the work of David Burns. We have consolidated some common negative self-talk phrases into a narrative of things that people might think or say about themselves with the words from the Burns list of ten "cognitive distortions" appearing in parenthesis. For the complete list and full descriptions see David D. Burns, *feeling good: the new mood therapy*. (Burns, 1980)

People often see things in black and white as all good or all bad (all or nothing thinking) with an emphasis on the bad. People can take a single event and turn it into an assured pattern of continuing defeat (overgeneralization). Some will put on dark glasses (mental filter) and dwell on the negative while failing to see or count constructive or beneficial occurrences (disqualifying the positive). Sometimes people will see a pattern in a small amount of evidence (jumping to conclusions) and use this as a crystal ball for making predictions about what's going to happen. Commonly, people will also see things in extremes, making matters much worse or better than they actually are (magnification and minimization), sometimes even turning a troubling minor event into a catastrophe. Reasoning can take a back seat to feelings (emotional reasoning) as feelings shape a false but defining picture of how things are. People will blame themselves and take more responsibility than warranted, using a lot of phrases such as I have to, I ought, I must (should statements) instead of I want to. People with negative thoughts will often put negative labels on themselves (labeling and mislabeling), in effect naming the character they are and acting out their part because that's the label they have. Sometimes when something bad occurs, people will take personal responsibility for it (personalization) when actually they are not primarily accountable. (Burns, D.,1980, pp.32-41)

It may be difficult at times for those who mourn to hold accurate views of themselves or the situation they are in during the high-stress experience of grief. It is a time at which distorted thinking habits might even become magnified. Becoming familiar with common thought distortions on the list by Burns and learning to identify which ones seem most applicable to oneself is a good place to start. Then the goal is to reconstruct irrational beliefs or distortions into healthier patterns to relieve emotional distress, which may require guidance from a counselor or someone asking: Do you really believe that? Is there another way to look at it? What's the evidence for that? What are the implications of believing that? With practice, this self-examination of one's self-talk can also be directed from within, once there is recognition of the need for it, by asking oneself those same questions.

Reconstructing perceptions and beliefs is not easy because sometimes they have deeper roots in a preestablished way of looking at the world called "schemas," and reworking them can take time and effort. (Malkinson, 2007, p.65) But grief provides an opportunity for doing that, learning how to rebuild maladaptive core beliefs and thinking habits while developing more inner control over the feelings associated with loss. Attitude matters in moving toward resilience.

GRIEF AND AGING

A loss brings concern about one's own mortality at any age, but older people in particular, for whom death may be closer in arriving, may be more preoccupied with dying. That can affect grieving. As Bonanno notes, "Fear and anxiety about the end of life are not uncommon." (Bonanno, 2019, p.176) At various stages of life, people cope with the prospects of their own mortality in various ways, including denial, distraction, and pushing such thoughts aside for later. But for older people who have experienced loss, denial of their own death is less likely. In fact, for them, one might say, grieving includes the task of terror management.

For the aging, reshaping self-talk about one's own mortality as a form of cognitive control, becomes especially important for manifesting and maintaining resilience. Bonanno reminds mourners that terror can also be contrasted with curiosity and shaped by satisfaction: "Soon I will know something that no living person knows…I will know what happens when we die." (Bonanno, 2019, p. 176) Well, yes, but the elderly are seldom dying to satisfy that curiosity.

Pet Loss Grief

Pets also have mortality. They don't live nearly as long as humans, but it is easy to get very attached to them in a short time. For those who have loved and lost their pet, they experience feelings in many ways comparable to the feelings of those who mourn human loss. The loss may be valued differently by some, of course, but the feelings of grief are shared almost universally. The loss of a pet is at least important enough for Herbert Neiburg and Arlene Fisher to have written a book about it called *Pet Loss*. (Neiburg and Fisher, 1982) As they point out, pets have an important place in many human lives; and strong attachments, parallel but different from human attachments, often develop. Pets frequently provide their owners with a sense of purpose and meaning as well as a consistent form of companionship, protection from intruders, and loyal loving bonds. They also offer an opportunity for regular outdoor exercise and are often a social asset in relating to others who have pets through classes, mutual walks, or dog parks. Dogs especially have an unusual kind of devotion, an uncritical love that is always there, regardless of the number of "treats" received that day. (Unconditional love may not always be so frequently observed in humans.)

All of this makes the process of grief for a pet parallel in some respects to human grief, yet distinct. Add to this the frequent dilemma of prescribed euthanasia, and the feelings of grief regarding the loss of a pet can be intense. This loss may be especially difficult for children and may be their first exposure to an awareness of death. Helping children grieve can be difficult for a parent who has also lost that pet.

Although the patterns of grief tasks have not been studied systematically with pets, one can see, just through observation, that grieving for a pet can be difficult and painful. The tasks outlined above may need some adaptation, but it seems reasonable to apply the tasks broadly to pet loss, including accepting the reality of the loss, processing the pain, adjusting to a world without the pet, and remembering and going on without the deceased pet. While maintaining the important value of human life, one can easily observe the parallels in patterns of grieving for humans and pets. (Nieburg and Fischer, 1982, pp. 3,8,45,47-55)

Things to Try

We have a general idea now of the tasks to be faced by those who grieve. We know that resilience is likely, but that complicated grief can occur. We know that self-talk needs to be positive. Older people may have an intensified view of their own mortality through grief. We are aware that the experience of grieving for family members or human companions can also apply to pets. But what is to be done? Will anything facilitate the adjustment to loss? The poet, Alfred Lord Tennyson, 1809-1892, puts the question well in *In Memoriam A.H.K.,* as cited in Moffat, 1992, p.260.

> O sorrow, then can sorrow wane?
> O grief, can grief be changed to less?

Will sorrow wane (diminish) or grief be changed to less? Yes, there is a good chance of that. There are things to do, to try, to experiment with, and see what effect they might have.

As we shift away from this more theoretical discussion of grief, we explore a list of activities and exercises that provide practical ways to tackle the tasks of grieving. The original sources of these activities are identified, but most have been expanded or reimagined as they are put in their present form here by the authors. Some activities may be more appropriate for the period of early grief, while others are better saved for later. They are intended for all kinship relations and types of loss and can be freely adapted for special circumstances and to address the tasks of grieving. Some of the suggestions on this list may have no appeal at all or will appear to be too time-consuming, unsuitable, or even upsetting. So, the goal is to select something that looks promising and explore it by adapting it and using it. A checklist is provided at the end for quick reminders. These activities may provide assistance in the search for ways to help sorrow wane or change grief to less.

ACTIVITIES

Services and Observances. Holding formal services, religious observances, or remembrance days produces descriptions of the deceased and enables conversations about loss. Having a graveyard service or place of remembrance for ashes provides an occasion for sharing memories of the deceased as well as serving as concrete, public acknowledgment of the loss. (Kessler, 2019, p.44) Sometimes a second service or day of remembrance can be held a year later as a memorial on the date of death. (Wolfelt, 2016, p.72)

Eulogies. Writing a eulogy that is balanced and respectful provides a brief picture of the life of the deceased and an organized list of those affected by the loss. Published or not, eulogies provide a snapshot of the life of the person who is gone. (Kessler, 2019, p.143)

Open House. Friends and neighbors can be invited to stop by at designated times during a specific week. Based on the Jewish practice of Shiva, a seven-day mourning period in which community members are expected to visit the mourner, a structured memorial invitation may be used to let acquaintances know that it is okay and comfortable for the mourner to talk about the loss. (Hagman, 2016, p.107)

Continuing Friendships. Continuing the friendships with people who had a special relationship with the deceased brings their perspective on that person and the loss *they* are experiencing. (Wolfelt, 2001, #33)

Legacy Book. A scrapbook can be created consisting of photos, clippings, and memorabilia that help to tell and illustrate the story of a life. This activity involves assembling an explicit vision of the essential characteristics of the deceased. (Hagman, 2016, p.xxxiv)

Online Legacy. This involves uploading a selection of memorable photographs and videos as an electronic scrapbook of memories, available to the mourner and others who knew the deceased. As a source for social media exchange, it can also be accessed by phone for convenient use or to show others. (Kessler, 2019, p.218)

Music Playlist. Attending live concerts or assembling an online playlist of the deceased person's favorite music, to be shared with others or enjoyed privately, can be a way of eliciting musical memory experiences of the deceased. (Davis and Robinson, the authors)

Photo Sharing. Sharing cherished photos of the deceased among family members may bring about family discussions and shared memories. Photo sharing can also be used with new acquaintances who had not met the deceased before their passing. It provides an opportunity to share more about their attributes and ways they are remembered. Photo sharing is an important and enjoyable vehicle of introduction in grief groups and can be used along with the sharing of other items as well, such as videos, clothing, or memorabilia of special interests or hobbies. (Worden, 2018, p. 108)

Sentimental Immersion. Spending time reading old cards, letters, emails, or watching home movies and videos, immersing oneself in sentimental memories is a sure way to elicit emotional catharsis. It has its legitimate time and place in the grief process. (Davis and Robinson)

Linking Objects. As many belongings, such as clothing, are removed from the place of residence, certain linking objects (a watch, jewelry, toys, sports equipment, travel souvenirs) are often retained as a special connection to the deceased. If the same residence is maintained, daily reminders are everywhere but keeping a few special objects that link to how the person lived and what they enjoyed may be especially meaningful. (Worden, 2018, pp.167-68, Kessler, 2019, p.215)

Letter Writing. Letters provide an imaginative format for communicating with the deceased even though that person doesn't receive the letters or have a way to reply. Letters provide a way to express feelings of longing or regret, and a sense of closeness is often experienced as the letter is being written. Sometimes an imagined response is also written as a reply from the deceased. Short notes are sometimes written to a deceased parent by a child. Actual letters or emails can be sent to friends or relatives, and old acquaintances are often renewed in this way. (Neimeyer, 2016, p.190, Kubler-Ross and Kessler, 2019, pp. 143-145)

Journaling. Using this popular way of keeping a diary provides those who grieve with a way of putting on paper the confusing thoughts going on in the head and the feelings churning in the heart. Journaling provides an opportunity for making sense of what's happening day-by-day and a way of monitoring self-talk and adaptation to grief over time. (Hagman, 2016, p.xxx)

Log of Feelings. Throughout a single day, feelings are recorded as a way to discover what experiences seem to be related to which feelings. What things seem to trigger anger, sadness, joy, loneliness, or a sense of agitation or calm? If the log is helpful, it can be repeated on another day, or several days, and used for comparison. (DeVine, 2017, p.93)

Brief Written Memories. Strong memories can turn into poems, paragraphs, or song lyrics. A mourner might ask what they miss most about the deceased, what images are the strongest, and why these memories surfaced. (Worden, 2018, p. 163)

Fictional Character. Writing can also take the form of a fictional short story with a main character who has experienced loss. The writer can draw on personal experience and project that onto the created character to see how that person acts on feelings and ideas. Grief gains a fictional voice for considering options and exploring what happens. (DeVine, 2017, p.157)

Drawing or Painting. Art can express feelings. Drawing or painting can contain concrete images of shared experiences or abstract representations of emotions, ranging from dark sadness to joyous bright remembrance. Art is another way to get grief out and into another form. (Worden, 2018, p. 108)

Gardening. Perhaps the deceased had a special attachment to a particular flower in the garden or certain indoor plants. Continuing to cultivate them or starting a new memorial garden can contribute to the experience of healing. (Wolfelt, 2002, #48)

Love Bursts. When the heart is bursting with love for the deceased, as if they were still alive, the feelings can be put into words or down on paper. Then certain words the beloved spoke in return are remembered as well as the acts of kindness they showed when they were still alive and bursting with love, too. Who would want to forget that? (Kessler, 2019, p.202)

Dreams. Dramatic dreams, or little fuzzy ones, can make a strong impression. They can be logged in a dream book, so as not to be forgotten, and then explored further by sharing interpretive ideas with others. If there are several dreams, they may have an underlying theme. What are they trying to say? (Worden, 2018, pp.175,177)

Pet Loss Tribute. Writing a short tribute can be a useful aid in adapting to the loss of a pet. This can be a few words for a real or imagined tombstone inscription, a creative poem, or a short letter that summarizes the essence of that pet's identity and the importance of the relationship. An online photo or video of a special memory may be included. For those who wish, holding a family memorial service may help bring closure to the loss and may offer children in the family an opportunity to talk about death as they memorialize the loss of their pet. (Nieburg and Fisher, 1982, p.68)

Bereavement Group. Good assistance and support with grieving can come through grief education or grief therapy groups under various types of leadership and sponsorship. Self-help bereavement groups also exist. Sometimes groups continue to meet after the scheduled sessions to continue sharing their experience in adapting to grief over time and extend the bonds of their new friendships. An effective way of learning from loss is to learn from the losses of others. (Rando, 1991, p.311) If no sponsored group is available, it may be appropriate to initiate an informal one. (Wolfelt, 2016, p.128)

Empty Chair. A person who has experienced loss can imagine the deceased sitting nearby in an empty chair. After expressing to them personal thoughts and feelings, it is possible to move into that empty chair and take on the role of the deceased, to imagine what they would say in return, speaking in their voice out loud. The empty chair is especially useful for dealing with unfinished business, guilt, or shame, but also for sharing progress or identifying unexpected events. (Worden, 2018, pp. 170,173)

Asking for Advice. Even though a loved one is gone, it is okay to ask what they would think or do about a particular situation. Losing a loved one often means losing a valuable consultant, but if the bereaved thinks to ask, advice may be readily available. Those who have lost parents often describe the sensation of having one or both still sitting on their shoulders ready to make suggestions. In a close relationship, the mourner usually knows what the deceased would think or do. Acting on that advice is another matter. (Rando, 1991, p.233)

Memorial Bench. Many parks and recreation areas welcome the donation of a bench containing a small plaque with the name of the deceased and the donor. The bench serves as a memorial but also as an alternative gravesite, a place to visit and remember the deceased. (Kessler, 2019, p.207) Parks may also welcome a memorial tree with a personal marker. (Wolfelt, 2001, #70)

Commune with Nature. Being away from domestic surroundings and immersed in nature's beauty can be restorative and even energizing. It may be a familiar walk once shared or a completely new location far from civilization, but a walk in the forest where the silence is broken only by the song of a bird or the rush of bubbling stream is often healing in a special way. Communing with nature can provide new perspectives on life and death and one's place in the natural world. (Wolfelt, 2001, #91)

Traveling to a Favorite Place. It can be painful to try to travel again to a place a loved one had cherished, but it can also be a trip of gratitude for having enjoyed a special place together. It is a way of trying to overlay sad memories of loss with happy memories of remembrance. (Kessler, 2019, p. 210)

Living Legacy. Honoring the memory of the deceased can also involve identifying certain likable qualities they had and then trying to exhibit these characteristics in the way one lives. If they had a positive attitude, a good sense of humor, or a special friendliness for new acquaintances, it may be possible to emulate those qualities in the way one lives. The emphasis is on positive qualities that might live on through imitation. (Kessler, 2019, p. 211)

Alternate Holiday Celebrations. People who have suffered a loss often dread the celebration of holidays, not only the emotionally fraught December holidays, but also birthdays, anniversaries, Valentine's Day, and other family traditions. One can opt out, but to avoid social isolation, it may be better simply to change the celebration to a different time, location, or manner of observance, from something that was always done to something new. A turkey dinner doesn't always need to include turkey. (Davis and Robinson)

New Achievement. A loss can generate a new level of energy and motivation, perhaps somewhat surprisingly, to take on a new project, complete an unfinished one, or raise the bar of accomplishment. Examples include further education, constructing something useful or beautiful, or playing in a sports tournament or running in a race—something done openly or privately as a memorial. (Davis and Robinson)

Teaching Others. Having learned from loss, some will wish to share what they have learned as a way of helping others who are trying to adapt. Keeping in mind that everyone's grief is somewhat different, sharing wisdom informally not only helps other mourners cope, but it also deepens one's own understanding of loss. Deeper learning often comes to teachers through teaching. (Wolfelt, 2001, #95)

Legacy Gifts. Financial gifts to causes or institutions that a loved one liked, or would have liked, can be made as legacy gifts. They are sometimes made "in memory of" and labeled that way, through a will, or designated gift while the person is still alive. This is a way of continuing to express a person's interests when they are no longer able to do so. (Kessler, 2019, p.205) It is also fitting to continue the volunteer work in which they were engaged. (Wolfelt, 2016, p.120)

Public Cause. Some mourners establish a public cause to honor the death of a loved one. This may be especially useful when the manner of death—murder, preventable accident, mass violence, or acts of terror—is exceptionally traumatic or unexplainable. In the face of absurdity and injustice, some people try to do something about it. They take up a cause, create an organization, lobby for better safety measures, or establish a foundation, something that provides a meaningful counter to a meaningless death. (Kessler, 2019, p.208)

Organ Donation. Some people who die, particularly at a younger age, may still have healthy bodies, depending on the cause of death. One way for that person to literally "live on," is through organ donation, giving vital organs to other people who need them to stay alive. Naturally, the wishes of the deceased must be respected within the context of other plans for the physical remains, but organ donation is another option for turning something unexplainable into something useful to others. (Kessler, 2019, p.149)

Agencies and Resources. A surprising number of agencies and resources exist nationally and locally for those adapting to grief. Comprehensive lists exist in books, such as *How to go on Living When Someone You Love Dies,* and others are updated or available online. (Rando, 1991, Chapter 12)

A summary list of these activities that may help is found in Figure 8 and can be used to assist in exploration and selection.

FIGURE 8

CHECKLIST OF ACTIVITIES THAT MAY HELP

___Services and Observances ___Eulogies ___Open House

___Continuing Friendships___Legacy Book ___Online Legacy

___Music Playlist ___Photo Sharing ___Sentimental Immersion

___Linking Objects ___Letter Writing ___Journaling

___Log of Feelings ___Brief Written Memories ___Fictional Character

___Drawing or Painting ___Gardening ___Love Bursts ___Dreams

___Pet Loss Tribute ___Bereavement Group ___Empty Chair

___Asking for Advice___Memorial Bench ___Commune with Nature

___Travel to Favorite Place ___Living Legacy

___Alternate Holiday Celebrations ___New Achievement ___Teaching Others

___Legacy Gifts ___Public Cause ___Organ Donation

___Agencies and Resources

Dialogue

Counselor: Did you find time to look at that list of activities I gave you at our last session?

Mourner: Oh, the list of things to try? Yes, it looks interesting. I didn't have a list like that at the time of my losses, but I noticed that I happened to do some of the things on that list.

Counselor: Really? Which ones?

Mourner: Well, as I mentioned last time, I had joined a grief education group, like you had on the list. Mine was sponsored by my hospice care providers, and it was very important to me.

Counselor: How so?

Mourner: The facilitator encouraged us to tell our stories, and it turned out that we all seemed to be very good at listening as well as speaking, so we became good friends, sharing the grief we had in common, even though we came from different employment backgrounds and faith traditions.

Counselor: What helped you most?

Mourner: Listening to the stories of others gave me perspective on my own loss. You can't believe how some of those people suffered, both in the experience of the death of their beloved, but also in grief for their loss. I realized that I was certainly not alone. Sooner or later we all cried in front of each other.

Counselor: So, you developed a special bond with the members through your grieving.

Mourner: We worked our way through the special tasks of grieving, at least enough to know what they were, and the facilitator gave us a list of our phone numbers and emails and suggested that we continue to meet if we wished. I didn't think that would work out, but that was three years ago, and we are still meeting!

Counselor: As friends or mourners?

Mourner: Both. We talk about everything now, but at some point, we always ask, "How are you doing?" We have all adapted in our own way, month by month, year by year, but we also know that certain feelings never go away.

Counselor: What else on that list did you do?

Mourner: I wrote letters to my Brazilian wife. I think I picked up the idea from a neighbor.

Counselor: Were you comfortable with the idea of letters?

Mourner: Not at first. I remember starting off my first letter with something like: I don't know your address, and I doubt this will reach you, but I want to tell you how much I miss you, so I'm writing to you even though it feels a little spooky to do so.

Counselor: I guess that could feel a little strange. How many letters did you write?

Mourner: I wrote about one per week for the first year. Then I stopped.

Counselor: What did the letters do for you?

Mourner: More than I expected. Besides having a way to express how much I was missing her, I was able to discuss memories and tell her how I was doing. I would write a paragraph and sob, then write another paragraph and sob some more.

Counselor: They were an outlet for your sadness. But also a way to reflect on how you were coping.

Mourner: Yes. I began to see that memories could be simultaneously happy and sad. The letter writing was also a vivid acknowledgment of the reality of her death, a concrete way of processing the pain, and a kind of memorial to her absence but continuing presence in my life.

Counselor: I can see how those letters were important. What else did you try?

Mourner: My friend's wife brought me a piece of music for the piano written by her Norwegian grandfather, a "Song Without Words." As I played it, I thought it was the saddest piece of music I had ever heard in my life. In my sorrowful state, in my first weeks of mourning, I felt I was well-equipped to give the song without words some words.

Counselor: Lyrics to match that sad song?

Mourner: I knew I would be talking to you today about what I have done about my grief, so I brought a copy for you.

Counselor: I'd like to see it.

> Love We Have Forever
> We were young when we fell in love,
> Always happy, full of joy.
> Yes, I still remember all the times
> that we enjoyed together.
> Oh, I miss you so. I hope you know.
> Walking together all around the lake we loved so much.
> And when I sleep now, I still feel your touch.
> I miss you so. Where did you go?
> Love we have forever, life it passes by.
> We knew how to be so happy then,
> So tell me why we all must die.
> Love we have forever, life it passes by.
> I still see your smile each morn I wake.
> It will be with me 'til I die.

Counselor: Oh, my gosh, that's beautiful, but so sad. I can feel your loss.

Mourner: Excuse me for a moment. That melody always brings tears to my eyes and it's playing now in my head. The song by itself is sad enough without my words. But I think writing those lyrics helped me move on through my most intense sorrow. On the other hand, that sad song makes me more fearful and anxious about my own mortality. I think that's happening as I grow older.

Counselor: Are there things you did more recently when your pain and sadness eased up a bit?

Mourner: We were great travel companions, and when she died, I was sure I would never travel again. She plunked her credit card down to buy our very first time-share at a resort in Mexico, and then we bought more because we wanted to go there more frequently. For her, Mexico was halfway, culturally and geographically, to Brazil, and she adored being there. How was I to go back after she died? After a few months and with the encouragement of family, I did.

Counselor: Did it make you sad or happy? Perhaps both?

Mourner: I had to find that out. I was afraid I would cry the whole time, and at first it was difficult when workers at the resort would greet me and say, "Where is Senora?" Gradually, I began to feel that she was not missing, but there in spirit with me, my inseparable companion. When I felt sad, I didn't cry. Instead, I thought of how I would never have known the blue sky and warm ocean breeze of Mexico if it had not been for her urging me to try it the first time.

Counselor: Now you are making me tearful, not so much from sadness, but being able to hear how it made you happy. It is a very touching memorial, that courageous trip you took.

Mourner: Speaking of memorials, I distributed some of her ashes in a favorite mountain valley and others at the edge of a beautiful nearby lake, and although that might have been what she wanted and what we had discussed, I needed something more tangible to visit. So, I made arrangements for installing a memorial bench in a park only a short distance from my house, and now I drive over there every morning, sun, rain, or snow, to walk my half mile around the park and stop to chat with her at the bench. I sheepishly told my friends in the grief group that I sometimes spoke out loud to her at the bench, and they jumped all over me for being so timid about that, saying, "Come on, we all talk to our beloved. It's okay."

Counselor: Not necessarily believing she is actually there but continuing to acknowledge her meaningful presence in your life.

Mourner: Yes, nicely put. She's with me in a lot of ways wherever I go, and I often think about her positive characteristics and try to emulate them.

Counselor: To be more like her. How?

Mourner: She was unusually friendly to everyone. Our friends at the time-share resorts in Mexico were not the other owners, but the staff. She had a unique way of taking them out of their roles and treating each one with respect as a person, giving them an uplifting dignity.

Counselor: No wonder they missed her. So, do you try to be more like her in some ways?

Mourner: I do. More friendly and out-going, more courageous in trying out new things, calmer about the future. I try to think less about my script—what I should do— and more about what she would do. Then I'm very thankful that I have such a positive model to remember. Not everyone does.

Counselor: It sounds like she continues to have a profoundly positive influence on you.

Mourner: Yes, and I am more awakened now to similar influences with my other losses. When my parents died, I began to remember them more frequently than when they were alive. Shameful, but true. Now I was on my own in this puzzling world, and I welcomed their advice. They always encouraged me to have a positive attitude. Yes, they seem to sit on my shoulders now, available with a mere nod from me. My brother is still my special counselor, and my blind and disabled daughter continues to be an inspiration to me as I face challenges in life that call for patience or persistence.

Counselor: People of many cultures similarly respect their ancestral voices.

Mourner: That's true, isn't it? These were all family, but I also lost a work colleague, my associate. I would go to his office after everyone else had gone home, and we would sit there talking about how things were going, but also our past, like building balsa wood models of World War II fighter planes. Then he was diagnosed with pancreatic cancer and kept working right up until about three weeks before he died. He had become such a good friend. I think his dedication to work and his drive to be productive in the face of adversity is something I admire and try to emulate to this day.

Counselor: And your first wife. How is she remembered now, so many years later?

Mourner: Her mastery of the piano was halted by her care for our handicapped daughter. For sure there was no time to practice the piano anymore. Is that why I play the piano so much now? Because I have time to practice or because it is my way of remembering her sitting there at that grand piano given to her by her parents—I still have it in my living room— being so dedicated to those composers. I'm not nearly as talented or advanced as she was, but I still enjoy being able, as she did, to bring to life from a few notes on a printed page the legacy of Beethoven, Grieg, or Debussy.

Counselor: It seems there are many ways for the deceased to live on in your life.

Mourner: They are losses but not lost. That's how I think about it.

REFERENCES

Bonanno, G.A. (2019). *The Other Side of Sadness: What the New Science of Bereavement Tells about Life After Loss.* New York: Basic Books.

Burns, D.D. (1999). *Feeling good: the new mood therapy.* New York: Harper Collins Publishers.

DeVine, M. (2017). *It's OK That you're Not OK.* Boulder, CO: Sounds True.

Hagman, G. (Ed.) (2016). *New Models of Bereavement, Theory and Treatment.* New York: Routledge.

Kessler, D. (2019). *Finding Meaning: The Sixth Stage of Grief.* New York: Simon & Schuster.

Kubler-Ross, E. and Kessler, D. (2005). *On Grief and Grieving: Finding the Meaning of Grief through the Five Stages of Loss.* New York: Scribner.

Malkinson, R. (2007). *Cognitive Grief Therapy: Constructing a Rational Meaning to Life Following Loss.* New York: W.W. Norton & Company.

Moffat, M.J. (1992). *In the Midst of Winter: Selections from the Literature on Mourning.* New York: Random House.

Nieburgh, H. and Fischer, A. (1982). *Pet Loss.* New York: Harper & Row.

Neimeyer, R. (2016). *Techniques of Grief Therapy: Assessment and Intervention.* New York: Routledge.

Rando, T. (1991). *How to go on Living When Someone You Love Dies.* New York: Bantam Books.

Wolfelt, A. (2001). *Healing Your Grieving Heart: 100 Practical Ideas.* Fort Collins, Co: Companion Press.

Wolfelt, A. 2016). *When Your Soulmate Dies.* Fort Collins, CO: Companion Press.

Worden, J. W. (2018). *Grief Counseling and Grief Therapy: A Handbook for Mental Health Practitioners,* Fifth Edition. New York: Springer Publishing.

LESSON 4

CONTEMPLATING AND ADAPTING TO A NEW LIFE

The focus of this Lesson is on the third task, adjusting to a world without the deceased. This includes both external and internal adjustments needed to build either a new life or modify one's old life significantly to accommodate the loss. It is often a long journey down a lonely path to an unknown destination. (See cover photo.)

Rebuilding can involve very different responses depending on the nature of the loss. As explained in Lesson 1, kinship associations (family relationships) are important mediators of grief. The tendency is to think mainly of the loss of a spouse because that is frequent, but it is also important to consider the adjustment of a child who has lost one or both parents, a sibling who has lost a dear sister or brother, or parents who have lost a child or children. These are clearly different situations, and for each loss the world has been shattered in a different way. Rebuilding it will also vary, and the suggestions mentioned in this chapter will need to be adapted to each specific situation. But there are some general things to consider, some common ideas to ponder, and things to do that may assist the mourner with the task of adjusting to the world without the deceased.

Perhaps we should begin, however, with Megan DeVine's reminder that "even though we want a roadmap, you can't make grief tidy or predictable" because there is no pattern, no linear progression. (DeVine, 2017, p. 31) She suggests that it is better to witness each other's pain without rushing in to clean it up. (DeVine, 2017, p. 60-61) Yet many in the midst of grief have strong inner impulses to rebuild in some way, as if building a new life is a natural part of being resilient. The World War II French/Algerian resistance fighter and existentialist author Albert Camus, 1913–1960, states succinctly the need for new beginnings in *YouthfulWritings,* as cited in Moffat, 1992, p.233.

The fall is brutal,
but we set out again.

Whatever the loss or how brutal the fall, many who mourn feel the need to get back on their feet and set out again.

Those who study grief notice that people who are adjusting to a world without the deceased seem to oscillate between a "loss orientation," a reflection on the death, and a "restoration orientation," focusing on new roles and goals in an "attempt to reaffirm or reconstruct a world of meaning that has been challenged by loss." (Hagman, 2016, p.xvii) This lesson focuses on restoration.

It is natural to want the old world back, but that won't happen. The challenge is to adapt to the new world that exists without the deceased by repairing the self and rebuilding a new sense of identity. (Rando, 1991, pp. 238,239) But at the same time, one must attend to mundane daily responsibilities within the immediate scope of one's experience.

The task of adjusting to a world without the deceased, therefore, involves two sub-tasks. The first includes what are called *external adjustments* to the immediate conditions that affect daily life. When a person dies, the circumstances of the person left alive are changed, sometimes only moderately, but often drastically. The second part of the task includes *internal adjustments* having to do with feelings and attitudes about one's own identity in this changed world. Sometimes this part of the task can be confusing and unnerving.

External Adjustments

Some aspects of building a new life have to do with external adjustments, changes in behavior and activities as opposed to adapting to inner feelings about being in a new situation. External adjustments usually involve things to do and decisions to make. How these matters are handled can influence inner feelings, but the focus of external adjustment is on the immediate surroundings of the mourner and the necessary actions to be taken to be able to live without the deceased.

As with other aspects of learning from loss, external adjustments depend on many mediating factors. People will be affected in different ways by the loss, but a common list of practical concerns will emerge rather quickly, not only for the mourner, but for other family members affected by them. The guiding question becomes: Who is responsible for which concerns and who is in a position to do something about them? This is especially important when children are involved.

External adjustments can be developed into a list of things to take into consideration, as presented below, and can be adapted as needed for the special circumstances of each loss. The list is assembled and elaborated from concerns mentioned briefly (sometimes only a word or phrase) in various books about grief, and no effort has been made to credit sources for this common and somewhat self-evident list of things to consider. Doing them, however, takes effort and good judgement.

Finances. What is the financial impact of the loss? Perhaps a source of income has been lost, or even a sole source of income. If there was a trust or will, its provisions need to be reviewed. Life insurance may provide extra income or fall short of what is needed. Perhaps the first external adjustment to make is to assess the immediate financial situation and make necessary adjustments in income and expenditure. In some cases, the adjustments may be minor or not required at all, but in others the loss can have significant and worrisome financial implications.

Housing. Does the loss impact housing and living conditions? It may or may not be possible to continue living in the same place of residence. Relocation may be necessary or desirable but probably won't work if used as escape from memories or feelings. If one stays in the same residence, choices need to be made about removing clothing, office equipment, and memorabilia of the deceased. The surroundings can be left more or less as they were, or significant remodeling can be undertaken.

Childcare. Does the loss affect the raising of children, stepchildren, or grandchildren? Responsibilities for children and arrangements for supporting and taking care of them will vary but must be agreed upon. Sometimes this involves shifts in residence or parenting with important implications for the child. With changing responsibilities, big implications can surface for children of all ages who are involved.

Occupation or Career. What implications does the loss have for the careers or occupations of those left behind? Sometimes these impacts are minimal even if the loss is shocking, but in other cases it may mean going back to work or even entering the employment world for the first time. Educational plans may be disrupted or modified. The balance of career and family responsibilities may need to be re-examined.

Domestic Roles. How will the household be managed? Housekeeping is usually broken into assigned or accepted roles. But now with the loss, certain roles may go unfilled and those left behind may or may not be capable of filling them. These include such things as shopping, cooking, cleaning, laundry, caring for the residence, and paying the bills. In today's world that may also include certain technology skills. Considerable adjustment is often required to learn new skills and play new roles. This may be welcome, viewed as daunting, or just accepted as a necessary responsibility.

Transportation. How is mobility affected? A loss may also involve the loss of a driver or the need for more transportation for those affected. Vehicle ownership and patterns of getting around may require change. Depending on the manner of death, driving may become something aversive. Some family members may be too young or too old to be on the road.

Social Support. With whom do the bereaved socialize? Old social patterns are often disrupted by a loss because a key person is missing. Although it may be difficult, maintaining a social support system is recognized as important. Old friendships dissolve as new ones appear. Sometimes previous acquaintances turn into important new friendships. Continuing to socialize even with familiar neighbors may now be difficult with an uncomfortable awareness of absence. Companionship is often an important alternative to loneliness, but how much is necessary, how deep does it go, and with whom?

Family System Impact. How is the family system as a whole impacted? Family members play roles, and this often includes differences in status and power. One person has stepped off stage, permanently, and that can affect how the family drama plays out, sometimes with a happy ending or with unresolved conflict and tension. Smoldering family relations, with the peacekeeper gone, can erupt in ugly battles full of deceit and hostility, resulting in deep dislike among certain family members bordering on hatred. Disagreements about finances are often the cause of family feuds. Most families, whether aware of it or not, function as systems with someone in charge and others going along. Loss can lead to open conflict and the need for restructured family relations. Sometimes this involves more than one family.

Health. What needs to be done to stay well in a world without the deceased? Although some deaths come as a traumatic shock, others are preceded by lengthy and difficult caregiving. A loss sometimes results in health implications for survivors, both mental and physical. Diet, rest, and sleep patterns are often disrupted. Some mourners resist putting time and effort into their own wellbeing and even wonder why they should continue living.

New Relationships. Should new personal or romantic relationships be formed? Age becomes a key factor in answering this question. Older people often say they are not interested; younger ones are often eager to do so. J. William Worden reports on one client "who picked out his new wife at his wife's funeral" (Worden, 2018, p. 103) New relationships depend on timing and can either lead to rebound marriages or newfound happiness. In some losses, such as a child or sibling, new relationships are not the point.

A checklist of these External adjustments is presented in Figure 9. The list can be used as a reminder of things that may need special attention considering the loss.

FIGURE 9

EXTERNAL ADJUSTMENT

A Checklist of Things to Consider:

______ finances

______ housing

______ childcare

______ occupation or career

______ domestic roles

______ transportation

______ social support

______ family system impact

______ health

______ new relationships

External adjustments usually result from necessity, but they can also be viewed as choices that provide opportunity. In any case, some significant changes often take place in the practical considerations of daily life as mourners adjust to a life without the deceased. New arrangements for living can result in huge adjustments or minor adaptations, depending on the loss. External adjustments can just happen or be well thought out, but they are usually not nearly as confusing and unnerving as internal adjustments.

Dialogue

Counselor: Remind me again of the adjustments you had to make to your life when your first wife died.

Mourner: The external adjustments were dramatic, but I had no list, no thoughtful way of approaching them. I had to buy groceries, put something together for dinner, do the laundry, attend the school meetings for special education students, and still prepare for my classes.

Counselor: You referred earlier to a sense of panic.

Mourner: Yes, as in, how can I possibly fit all of these new duties into my already busy life? Looking back now, it feels like I was just jumping from one thing to another without much thought, planning, or prioritization.

Counselor: Caught up in confusion?

Mourner: Yes, with a touch of desperation that led to bad decisions. I seemed to think that my external adjustments could all be solved by finding a new mother for my handicapped kid.

Counselor: But you managed somehow.

Mourner: I stayed in the same house, worked hard at my job, tried to comfort my blind daughter when kids picked on her at school, did the home chores, and remained in good health. My older daughter went on to the university and became very successful there, and I made conscious efforts to find out if she was happy and adjusting okay.

Counselor: You made a lot of satisfactory adjustments.

Mourner: Well, yes, I guess I did. It took a while to discover what wasn't working, mainly, my unreasonable expectation for a new mother for my handicapped daughter. I probably had more external adjustments associated with my divorce than with my loss.

Counselor: But that's a different kind of loss.

Mourner: Indeed. A few years before my divorce, my parents died, and as we speak of external adjustments, I remember my father.

Counselor: What do you recall?

Mourner: When my mother died at age ninety-two, my dad was left with a lot of adjustments that became challenging for him. Gender roles were sharply defined at the time—my mother didn't even drive a car—and although dad was a good breakfast cook, I don't think he knew much about lunch or dinner, and even less about the laundry. I remember his complaining about something called Meals on Wheels, as he struggled to live alone in that same house. If he had a list of external adjustments, it would have been long. I think he only lived for a year. I wish now, looking back, that we had helped him more to adapt, but it was tricky being clear across the country from him.

Counselor: He struggled through, largely on his own?

Mourner: Yes, and must have been lonely, too.

Counselor: And when your wife from Brazil died, many years later, was that different for you?

Mourner: Yes, there weren't many external adjustments apart from domestic chores and trouble-shooting computer problems. I stayed in my house, remodeling it slightly, and lived off my retirement income in solitude. But my internal adjustments were very difficult and daunting. I'll tell you about them next time.

INTERNAL ADJUSTMENTS

In Lesson 2 we explored the various kinds of feelings aroused in grief and learned how to express them by telling the backstory of the deceased, the event story of their death, and the deep feelings experienced during the early weeks of grief, the story of loss. The feelings usually include a deep sadness, and processing the pain of those feelings by expressing them is an important task of grieving. But something deeper may be going on underneath those feelings. In many cases, the loss not only evokes strong feelings; it has a larger impact on the self. Why do people say, "It feels like I lost a part of myself?"

ATTACHMENT

Relationships vary, and we know they can be close or distant, happy or stressful, intense or casual, with high and low impact, and that sometimes they are ambiguous and unclear. Through these variations, even in relationships that are sometimes stressful or ambiguous, there runs an attraction sometimes referred to as *attachment*. That connection, often beginning as mere attraction, can grow into an attachment with serious bonds. A strong attachment, when broken, will likely lead to painful grief. Why?

What is attachment and how does it affect grief? A chapter by Katherine Shear in Robert Neimeyer's *Techniques of Grief Therapy* explores the nature and impact of human attachment. Shear describes an attachment relationship as "involving two people who find it rewarding to be together and prefer not to be separated and who provide each other with comfort and solace when one of them is feeling badly and serve as coaches and cheerleaders when things are going well." (Shear in Neimeyer, 2016, p. 15) Note how this insightful definition can apply to couples but also to parents and children as well as siblings. Shear points out that as humans we seem to be "biologically disposed to seek, form, and maintain attachment relationships throughout our lives and to respond to their loss." (Shear in Neimeyer, 2016, p. 15) Making attachments is a normal thing to do and we do it knowing that we can suffer if something happens to that relationship. Suffering is not a sufficient reason to avoid attachments.

Consider how the theme of loss is expressed in so many popular love songs, usually as breakup or abandonment, and how that theme becomes tragic when the loss is through death. As Shear summarizes it: "Plainly put, the people we love define who we are so when we lose them, we are confused about our very selves, disoriented, and lost." (Shear in Neimeyer, 2016, p. 15) Losing someone with whom there is a close attachment has a profound impact on the self.

Attachment theory grew out of the study of children and parents, where the emotional need of children is for security and safety. Young children often reach out to explore the world a bit but then return to attach to parents again for basic needs. Attachment has been observed in the behavior of the young with their parents in almost all species of mammals. Attachment behavior has also been observed in adult species of geese and in ostrich mates, elephants and orcas, among others. Humans can become attached to animals as well, as we have noted with pet loss. In adults, attachment is often expressed as bonds of affection. (Worden, 2018, p. 16)

People vary, of course, in their degree of attachment, sometimes referred to as *attachment style*. The attachment bonds between adults are different from the attachment of parents and children, mainly because adult attachment is usually mutual, and both partners "serve as an attachment figure to each other." (Worden, 2018, p. 68) The amount of closeness will vary, and not all attachments are healthy and satisfying. Some involve ambivalence, exploitation, or at the extreme, abuse and co-dependence. Adult attachments are usually influenced by patterns experienced in childhood. As Worden points out, "healthy attachments, when broken, lead to feelings of grief. (Worden, 2018, p. 71) Not only sadness, but severe disorientation can occur. Why?

The Self

Does everyone have a self? There is a controversy about that, depending on what is meant by the word *self*. Some theoretical paradigms suggest that there is no such thing as a permanent self, offering as proof that the mid-life self is nothing like the teenage self. Most would agree with the example. Lacking permanence, the self may, however, exist at particular periods in time, enduring long enough to be influenced by another self.

If there is no such thing as the self, it is surprising to find in the dictionary more than three pages of hyphenated "self-words," such as self-control, self-denial, self-educated, self-esteem, self-help, selfish and selfless, as well as self-worth. If the self does not exist, language, nonetheless, has many words to describe it. Let's assume, for the purpose of discussion, that human beings may have an aspect of their being that might reasonably be called "the self."

The self, assuming it exists, is shaped by many things, including inner attitudes and certain high impact events. Many psychologists, however, would say that the self is shaped and formed primarily through the influence of other selves. People can have a deep influence on each other, self upon self, to the point that one can experience, refer to, and describe the shaping of oneself (one's self) by another. Two selves can become enmeshed, entangled, woven together, interlaced, and entwined. This entwining or merging of selves may also be thought of as "an overlap in our identities," where *we* becomes more important than *you* and *me*. It is no wonder that when a beloved person dies, we wonder who we are. Consider this extreme example: If the mother of an only child experiences the death of the child, is she still a mother? Identity is deeply affected by the merging of selves and subsequent loss. (O'Connor, 2022, p. 36) Through this connection of selves, certain attributes of one self begin to impact the other self. People grow, develop, and change as a result of the influence of an *other*.

When people's lives become entwined, whether as spouses, children and parents, grandparents and grandchildren, or as siblings, that person, the other, has become a part of the self, and losing that person when they die is like losing a part of the self. That loss brings damage to the self because it may be experienced as losing not only the deceased, but important parts of the self that were shaped by the deceased. (Hagman, 2016, p. 117) Through personal interactions, the influence of the deceased has become so strong as to exist as an actual part of the mourner's self. The things they did served the emotional needs of the self, and sometimes those things became special because they took priority over that person's own needs. More simply, we might call it love or affection. When a person dies, there is often a "loss of affection that was important to shaping and maintaining the self of the person who continues to live." (Hagman, 2016, p.115) One might say, when an important source of love and affection disappears, the self itself is often severely damaged by that loss. The death of a loved one, therefore, can be experienced as a "self crisis." (Hagman, 2016, p.118)

A major part of the internal adjustment in grieving is addressing this "self-crisis." The sense of having lost a part of one's self becomes a reality. Adjusting to a world without the deceased now also involves adjusting to a world with fragments of one's own self floating unmoored, aspects of one's identity badly shaken up, and the foundations of one's "self-esteem" severely compromised. "Who am I now?" becomes a serious and consuming question as the mourner begins to realize "I am not who I was." The task of building a new life by making certain external adjustments, while still important, is somewhat diminished as the mourner faces the very difficult internal adjustments of rebuilding the self.

The first step in addressing the "self-crisis" is to be aware of it, to understand it, and to find some words and images to describe one's own particular version of it. One might ask: What *aspects* of the self are most affected? In every person and relationship certain aspects of the self are more prominent and more influential than others. Consider, for purposes of discussion, that a person may have a work-world self, domestic self, cultural self, technology self, social self, hobby self, political self, spiritual self, charitable self, an athletic aspect of the self that enjoys activity or another part of the self that enjoys solitude. Obviously, substitutions or additions can be made to this illustrative list to tailor it to the unique identities of those who are involved. The key questions to ask are: What aspects of the self were most prominent and important in this relationship? How did the different aspects of the two selves touch and influence the mourner and the deceased? Which aspects of these two selves became deeply entwined?

A mourner without words or mental images to help describe this "self crisis," may remain confused about internal adjustment and how to respond adequately. It may be too dramatic to say that an entire self has been shattered, and more accurate to suggest that specific shared aspects of the self require repair and rebuilding. The challenge is to put the remaining pieces back together again.

Repairing the Self

Does the self have the capacity to repair itself? Can a person plant seeds in the midst of winter and expect them to grow? The famous American poet, Emily Dickinson, 1830–1886, once wrote these lines, as cited in Moffat, 1992, p.1.

> Winter under cultivation
> Is as arable as spring.

Most crops can't be grown in the winter, but the key word is *cultivation*, which implies plowing, planting, and tending, in other words, working at it, doing what will support growth, making winter as suitable for growing crops (arable) as spring.

The first step in repairing the self is coming to terms with memories. Memories of the deceased are inevitable. Some people cherish these memories; others find them disturbing and would like to be free of them. Most people like to think that they search for memories and are in charge of recall, even though what they try to remember is not always retrieved. The recall that people initiate often functions, but neuroscience tells us that they are not always fully in charge. People also have involuntary memories that come up spontaneously (perhaps uninvited), and those memories can be disruptive. Perhaps the deceased comes into view or is "suddenly there in our mind." Mourners are working hard to accept the death as real and final, but the brain is also working hard, like an old friend, still trying to catch up and figure out what has happened as with the disrupted mental mapping described in Lesson 2. It is difficult to accept the finality of the loss when the brain continues to send realistic reminders of the deceased. (O'Connor, 2022, pp. 126-130)

Can we control involuntary memories? We can try, but some neuroscience studies suggest that the more we try to avoid thinking certain things, the more they are thought about unintentionally. Higher cognitive avoidance seems to invite more intrusive thought. (O'Connor, 2022, p.183) Suppressing memories of the deceased may create more of them. It's not easy to manage the brain. It may be better to be aware of memories, intentional or not, accept them, learn to live with them, and find a positive place for them.

Another type of memory to watch for is a hard-to-manage sense of longing called *yearning.* The mourner wants to be with the deceased and has trouble letting go of cherished memories of being together. It is natural to want to be with the beloved, even though they are gone, but intense yearning can shut down more positive efforts to repair the self. Once again, the brain is catching up, sending a multitude of reminders. (O'Connor, 2022, p. 126-130)

Another memory hazard is called *rumination,* a word used to describe the process of going over and over something in the mind. The idea of repetition is caught in the second definition of that word, which refers to a cow or sheep chewing its cud. That is also rumination. Oddly enough, when people are anxious about the future, they tend to ruminate about things in the past, particularly something they wish they hadn't done. People who mourn can easily fall into the pattern of rumination, chewing their cud about something that is probably not going to aid in building a new self. Grief-related rumination tends to focus on a few unresolved issues associated with the loss. There is a tendency to supply long and detailed explanations of why something happened. Psychologists think of rumination as an avoidance process, a defense against having to face and resolve deeper issues of grief. (O'Connor, 2022, p. 153-156)

O'Connor suggests two ways of responding to rumination that we believe might also apply to yearning and involuntary memories. A person's response can be either *brooding* or *reflection.* Brooding is a repetitious mental pattern that goes nowhere. (O'Connor, 2022, pp. 147-48) Reflection involves thinking about the causes of these repetitive patterns, examining them, and making plans for doing something about them. Managing memories is a big challenge, especially the emotion-laden memories associated with loss, but managing memories in positive ways is better than being at their mercy or simply discarding them. Reflection is the beginning of finding a positive place for memories in repairing the self.

The task of building a new life involves both remembering and planning, referred to as *retrospection* and *prospection.* When brain scans are given to people who are remembering the past and imagining the future, there is significant overlap in the brain regions used for these functions. (O'Connor, 2022, p. 194) The brain is comfortable in doing both things, suggesting that it is not necessary to forget the past to be able to plan for the future. In fact, the challenge of building a new life involves incorporating the past into the future.

One way to begin to repair the self is by asking "Who was I before this happened?" What aspects of myself have not been disturbed and seem to be secure? What aspects of the self were intertwined and deeply enmeshed with the deceased? The recommended approach for repair today is not through withdrawal and disengagement with the deceased but by continuing to build that relationship. "Attachments to the deceased that are maintained rather than relinquished have been called continuing bonds." (Worden, 2018, p. 5) These involve positive memories. Odd as that advice for repair may sound, it has strong support today, but it takes cultivation.

Is it okay to have a continuing relationship with the deceased? Bonanno suggests that the value of it relates to timing. If the closeness exists in early mourning, it may be detrimental rather than helpful. Research suggests that "later is healthier." (Bonanno, 2019, p. 211) When the mourner has faced the reality of the death and takes on other tasks, the continuing relationship may become more comfortable, helpful, and enjoyable.

How does the mourner continue the relationship with the deceased? This is sometimes manifested by talking to the deceased, creating a sense of their presence, carrying on the beliefs, values, and causes of the deceased, and taking on some of the characteristics of that person. (Worden, 2018, p. 5) Some people find it very satisfying to keep the relationship going and even continue to develop it through imitative actions or memorializing commitments. Of course, an important way to continue that relationship is through memories.

The antidote to withdrawal is to encourage continuing memories of the deceased. Memories don't have to be accurate. Research suggests that they seldom are. Instead, it is what we do with our memories, how we handle them, and what they do for us. It is possible and easy to visit the deceased through memories, and in that way, the relationship is not completely gone. (Bonanno, 2019, pp. 104-107) In other words, the person is gone, but the relationship continues through memories.

In some cases, however, the death was so oppressive and shocking that memory of the deceased is extremely painful. The caregiving and death can produce stress and exhaustion, and watching the loved one suffer and decline in their capacities can have a kind of unforgettable misery attached to it. When the struggle is over, there is a "relief pattern" of forgetting. The same might be said for a stressful or ambiguous relationship. In these situations, it may take considerably longer to have positive memories, to be relieved of troublesome images, and to get beyond the guilt of feeling relief. Eventually, though not in all cases, it may be possible to continue that relationship as well. Death opens new doors for remembrance even when grief involves relief. (Bonanno, 2019, pp. 125-128)

The challenge is to "move to a new life without forgetting the old" and to continue the old relationship but in a new way. (Rando, 1991, p. 232-233) This happens by remembering, not forgetting, by appreciating the life you had together, recalling old routines and happy moments together, reliving travel adventures, and maybe even learning more about the deceased through things they have left behind. Perhaps continuing that relationship involves imagining how the person would have grown older had they lived longer. (Rando, 1988, pp. 235-238)

Reminders of various ways to continue the relationship are provided in the Checklist for Building Continuing Bonds, Figure 11. Some items on the list may be more attractive than others, so selecting some and trying them may be the best approach.

FIGURE 10

CHECKLIST FOR BUILDING CONTINUING BONDS

______ talking to the deceased

______ creating a presence

______ carrying on beliefs and values

______ taking on characteristics

______ imitating their actions

______ memorializing them

______ retaining happy memories

______ recalling old routines

______ appreciating the life lived together

______ remembering travel adventures

______ learning more about the life of the deceased

______ imagining growing older

Resilient mourners may walk the lonely path of rebuilding and restructuring life in a changed world, by making external and internal adjustments. Despite this, the consensus seems to be that sad feelings and painful memories never go away completely. Author Geoge Bonanno relayed that a client once told him that grief is like a fire that won't go out; if you blow on the glowing embers, they flicker and become bright again (Bonanno, 2019, p. 295) Grief, then, is not a fire to be put out but a means of adapting to the inevitable flicker. Setting out again. Winter under cultivation.

DIALOGUE

Mourner: Thank you for inviting me to meet you in the park today for some walk-and-talk counseling. This is new for me, so I don't know quite what to expect.

Counselor: Oh, I often counsel this way, and most clients say they prefer it to sitting in my office on that chair directly across from me with that clock ticking on the wall behind them. They say there is something about walking side by side that makes talking easier.

Mourner: And the fresh air is nice. Look how the path trails along by that beautiful river, and with that sunshine and blue sky as a backdrop. Now that you seem to know me a little better, I feel more comfortable just letting my thoughts and feelings flow like that river.

Counselor: Oh, I'm glad you feel that way. What did you want to talk about today?

Mourner: Before I tell you about the internal adjustments related to the loss of my Brazilian wife, I need to share the memories associated with the loss of my handicapped child.

Counselor, Yes, you told me that she died later in life in a painful death with ovarian cancer.

Mourner: I have many sad memories of that, watching her suffer serious and unrelenting pain, but also watching her unfulfilled life slip away. As I mentioned before, she completed college and graduate work. But then things fell apart for her as emotional problems developed—maybe from that earlier damage to her brain, the intensity of her therapies, or the loss of her mother as a teen—and it became clear that she could not live alone. At first, she struggled to do that and to hold a job, to be independent, through what I had often referred to as a twenty-year adolescence, but it eventually became necessary for her to enter an assisted living facility.

Counselor: So, we might say that when she was fighting her cancer, she was losing a life she was never able to live fully.

Mourner: So true. Whatever a "normal" life is, she wasn't able to live it because of being blind and having diminished mobility due to cerebral palsy, as they call it. Her story starts well, and in the middle she progresses, but the ending is so sad with a heap of unfair burdens and challenges to top it all off. So much was unfulfilled. Sometimes I am glad her mother was spared from watching it.

Counselor: Can you remember your daughter in a positive way now?

Mourner: I had a lot of dedicated support from her older sister, who visited regularly, and from my niece, but it was a relief when she finally died to see her suffering end. The memories of her suffering kept coming to me over and over, and I had trouble controlling that. It took me a long time to have positive memories.

Counselor: What was your attachment relationship like with her?

Mourner: Yes, we were attached in a somewhat complicated way. It was very difficult to raise her, and not always enjoyable for either one of us, with a continuation of parenting throughout her entire lifespan. We were both ambivalent about it, but the attachment was strong because I had put so much energy into it, and she depended on me and valued the security of my support without her mother.

Counselor: You're saying you have more than just sad memories of her, but sad memories, due to your unusual attachment, tended to dominate, at least for a while.

Mourner: Yes, so my task was not to disentangle the relationship, but to build a different one by remembering positive things about her through photos of her childhood, her stuffed animals, a locket she wore, and her braille watch. Remembering her helps me to adapt to her loss, but I'm still working on it.

Counselor: Have you had to change the way you think about her?

Mourner: Yes, I know that she would not agree with my view of her life as unfulfilled. I realize that's my own projection. Odd as it may seem, I don't think she thought of herself as unfulfilled. She found many ways to be happy: to sing, to laugh and joke around, and to take the bus service for the handicapped to meet friends for lunch. So, now I try to remember her happiness and it helps me with my sad memories. And you know what, sad as her story is, I can't imagine what it must be like to lose a young child through a horrible accident or some unexpected disease or a school shooting.

Counselor: I'm suspecting that raising her and looking after her later on involved a huge amount of investment in time and emotional energy from you. When she died, did you notice a void in that part of yourself? The caretaker?

Mourner: Thanks for bringing that to my attention. I don't think I've thought enough about that. But it's true. I was in effect a caregiver all of her life. It was part of my self-identity. Perhaps I just continued that aspect of myself because I was already caring for a new wife and her daughter, but in a much less demanding way since we were all happy and healthy. But then later, there I was again in that role as caregiver for my wife in the six months preceding her death.

Counselor: You were going to tell me about the internal adjustments to the loss of your wife.

Mourner: You mentioned attachment. How did we become so attached? I think I told you that for the entire first year, we called each other on Friday night, wrote long letters back and forth, and visited each other in our distant countries. I was a bit confused from my recent divorce, and my little Brazilian friend was finally breaking out of an unsatisfying relationship with the father of her daughter, so it was not so surprising that the two of us fell head-over-heels in love. But we both knew that was risky, and that we needed to calm down and become fully acquainted.

Counselor: Exactly what two highly rational professors do when they fall in love.

Mourner: Oh, look at those two birds chasing each other. They don't seem to have any reservations like I did.

Counselor: Well, you had good reasons for being careful.

Mourner: But look at how our deep acquaintance strengthened our attachment. She saved all those letters, mine and hers, in two notebooks and organized them chronologically. A few weeks ago, I reread them all. Now there's an experience: reading a candid and detailed record of our love story. I was stunned at how we cultivated such a deep attachment.

Counselor: Not mental memories, but an actual documented account in writing of how it happened at the time it happened?

Mourner: Yes, and that was just the beginning. It set in motion what was to become thirty years of attachment. By the time we got married at the end of that first year, we knew how to build that relationship by sharing everything, and we did that through the years that followed. There is an old Peter, Paul, and Mary folksong called "Follow Me" that uses the words: "make a part of you to be a part of me." Well, that's what we did. And then…then…

Counselor: I sense where this is going. Losing her shattered your sense of self.

Mourner: Two people had become one. So close that it was hard to tell who was who. We had a strong respect for each other's individuality, but that seemed to make it even easier to bond in the areas where her self touched mine, which was nearly everywhere. Then she became incurably ill.

Counselor: Two people closely entwined. And which aspects of the self were most seriously affected by the loss?

Mourner: I would say my cultural self. We both loved classical music, in concerts as well as recorded. Our house was simply but beautifully decorated with artwork on the walls and hand-woven Mexican throw rugs on the wood floors. We attended Broadway musicals downtown and in New York City, and we watched old classic films from her extensive CD collection. We also shared aspects of our domestic and political selves and watched TV news together. Now that she is gone, some important aspects of my self are gone, too. I haven't adapted very well to losing those parts of myself. At times I feel like a half-empty glass that will never be refilled.

Counselor: Sometimes that closeness is irreplaceable. How did you handle that?

Mourner: Not very well. Even though her daughter and I took care of her for six months, knowing she was dying, when it happened, I was completely shocked by the loss and the impact it was having on me. I felt unprepared emotionally and sobbed continually.

Counselor: Yes, having such a strong attachment makes the adjustment especially difficult, but it makes sense that despite knowing that the end of her life was looming, it still felt like a shock when it happened.

Mourner: In terms of my adjustment, I wrote her letters after she died, like I told you, but I also tried to get comfortable with memories, trying to remember her living her life instead of the period leading up to her death. I recalled our daily routines, our travels, our listening to music together. I even began to remember *her* memories. Her favorite one was sitting on her father's lap as a little girl on their sugar plantation in Brazil listening to Beethoven on the best available imported "hi-fi" player at the time. They were especially close because she was born on her father's birthday, but her father died of that family heart condition when she was nine years old.

Counselor: Oh, no, her experience of loss began when she was that young? So, tell me about that grief group you mentioned. Did that help with adapting to the loss of someone so close?

Mourner: Yes, a lot. At first we shared our stories, but later on we had a session devoted to building a new life. I listened for a while and then I said, "This is okay for all of you who are quite a bit younger than I am, but for me, hey, at my age, this is ridiculous." One woman in the group jumped on me in that gentle manner we had all developed with each other. "Come on," she said, "my mom lived to be one hundred and four. You could have a long life ahead of you. Are you just going to sit there and sob?"

Counselor: So direct but really on target. What did you do?

Mourner: I made some efforts to build a new life. I started down the lonely path to an unknown destination. After years and years of taking care of family members, I was suddenly free of that and could begin to think about next steps. I cultivated friendships with my former colleagues, going out to lunch or having them over for a summer cookout. One couple who I didn't know well became my close friends. I started writing again and playing the piano more. As I mentioned, I even traveled back to Mexico.

Counselor: The bubbling stream and that tall maple tree are reminding me that we should probably turn back here, retrace our steps along this path, so to speak. You were telling me how you have been building a new you from the old you. How did that work out?

Mourner: Fairly well. But sometimes I questioned those efforts. I remember saying to my oldest daughter on the phone one night that as I tell you all these things I'm doing, I sometimes wonder what the point of it all is. Are these friends really enjoying spending time with me or are they just doing this out of sympathy? Well, shame on me for questioning that, but when I compared the new life to the old, it didn't feel as deep or enjoyable as spending time with my dear wife when she was alive and well. I still missed her, and I felt like a piece of myself was still missing. I was starting to think that maybe I shouldn't be having her on my mind so much, but then one night I was reading a book on grief, and I learned about "continuing bonds" and how it was not only okay but to be encouraged to continue building that relationship with my wife and to remember her and even talk to her.

Counselor: So, you started doing that?

Mourner: I did. Every morning when I went for a walk, I stopped at her memorial bench, the one I told you about in the park, and we'd have a little chat.

Counselor: About what?

Mourner: Well, first of all, the weather. Isn't that how people usually start a conversation? Being from Brazil, she hated the cold winter but loved the sun and blue sky. So, I started out by describing the sun and the sky to her. Then I'd mention the family, her daughter and the grandchildren. Sometimes I'd tell her what I was planning for the day. With things that were bothering me, I asked her what she would do. I always told her how much I missed her.

Counselor: Why do you think that helps?

Mourner: Because she doesn't seem "totally gone." I can come into her presence with thoughts and feelings we often shared. Then that aspect of myself isn't so "gone" either.

Counselor: And your daughter, your stepdaughter, that is, how does she deal with memories of her mother?

Mourner: She speaks positively of various recollections of her mother. But listen to this, she also has involuntary reminders that she is her mother's daughter. She notices that she holds her hands in little curled up fists as her mother did, that she sometimes speaks to her children as her mother would speak to her, or that she is sitting in front of her computer with the same posture that her mother once did.

Counselor: So that her memories of her mother live on in the mannerisms and movements of her own body. And are these favorable reminders of her mother's influence?

Mourner: Oh, yes, she says she will always remember her mother because she is like her mother so much that even small physical movements remind her of her mother's presence in herself, not so much as a memory, but as a bodily presence.

Counselor: Was this disturbing or comforting to her?

Mourner: She seems to have incorporated that physical presence into her life in a positive way, so that she enjoys noticing her mother in herself, so I would assume comforting.

Counselor: Perhaps you notice the resemblances as well, which can also trigger memories of your wife.

Mourner: Yes, sometimes I see her there in her daughter, too. It makes me smile.

Counselor: Does she also have what we would call ordinary memories of her mom?

Mourner: She says that memories of her mother come flooding back most intensely when she is being a mother herself. I'm mothering the kids, she says, and that reminds me of my mother mothering me.

Counselor: Her mother, of course, was a self with many aspects, but her daughter remembers best the part of her that was her mother.

Mourner: Yes, she says that while she is doing something for her children she flashes back into a time in her house in Brazil when she was a child and her mother was helping her with her schoolwork, taking her swimming or to the open market, or when her mom was in her little office preparing for her classes at the university. And she wonders how her mother could have done all of that, holding two jobs and being a single parent.

Counselor: So, the aspects of those two selves that touched most intensely were as daughter and mother, and that's what is most naturally remembered.

Mourner: Yes, for the daughter, now in her early forties, the most salient aspect of her loss, is of her mother as a devoted and caring mother, whereas for me, as her mother's spouse, different aspects of the self, mine and hers, touched each other and entwined to bring forth for me in my grief different sorts of memories from those of her daughter.

Counselor: Yes, that makes sense. It's an interesting example of how grief touches different aspects of the self in different ways. Oh, there's my favorite bench here. Let's sit for a minute and review where we are. It seems you have adapted to your loss by building a new life, or perhaps we should say that you rebuilt your old life, by connecting with former colleagues, turning acquaintances into new friends, getting comfortable with memories, staying in touch with your daughters and their children, travelling, playing the piano, continuing to write, and by talking to her. And do you think that might please her?

Mourner: Yes. I can see her smiling and nodding her head with approval and support. I notified a mutual friend of ours in Mexico when she died, and she emailed me, "Try to be happy because that will make her happy."

Counselor: And are you happy?

Mourner: I'm getting there. After rereading our letters, I became aware of how important happiness was in her life and how she found it in so many different places.

Counselor: And that inspires you to be happy?

Mourner: Especially when I see blue sky and sunshine, like today, out here walking the path by this river. She loved the sunshine. I used to tease her about worshipping the Aztec Sun God, but she always reminded me that she was Catholic. We can talk more about that next time.

REFERENCES

Bonanno, G.A. (2019). *The Other Side of Sadness: What the New Science of Bereavement Tells about Life after Loss.* New York: Basic Books.

DeVine, M. (2017). *It's OK That You're Not OK.* Boulder, CO: Sounds True.

Hagman, G. (Ed.) (2016). *New Models of Bereavement, Theory and Treatment.* New York: Routledge.

Moffat, M.J. (1992). *In the Midst of Winter: Selections from the Literature on Mourning.* New York: Random House.

Neimeyer, R. (2016). *Techniques of Grief Therapy: Assessment and Intervention.* New York: Routledge.

O'Connor, M-F. (2022). *The Grieving Brain.* New York: Harper Collins Publishers.

Rando, T. (1991). *How to go on Living When Someone You Love Dies.* New York: Bantam Books.

Worden, J.W. (2018). *Grief Counseling and Grief Therapy: A Handbook for Mental Health Practitioners,* Fifth Edition. New York: Springer Publishing.

LESSON 5

MAKING MEANING AND EXPLORING TIMELESS QUESTIONS

The first task of grief is accepting the reality of the loss. For those who are able to do this, the fact of death becomes certain. A well-known author of religious reflections, C.S. Lewis, 1898–1963, expresses that reality in his book *A Grief Observed,* as cited in Moffat, 1992, p.115.

> I look up at the night sky. Is anything more certain
> that in all these vast times and spaces, if I were allowed
> to search them, I should nowhere find her face, her voice,
> her touch? She died. She is dead. Is the word so difficult to learn?

Death brings certainty, but perhaps the only thing that is certain in loss is the death itself. Beyond that singular certainty is a mourner's mind full of unanswered questions and unresolved mysteries.

Loss raises a lot of questions and humans want answers. Why did *they* die? How could a loving God let this happen? Could it have been prevented? Is some aspect of the deceased still living on in spirit? Why do people have to die? Is life totally pointless? Discussions in otherwise helpful books on grief usually stop short of addressing these questions, and the mourner lives on unassisted, trying to sew together a patchwork of explanations for unanswered questions. We acknowledge and try to address these questions in Lesson 5.

The focus of this lesson, however, is not on answering these questions but on providing a guide for thinking about them. The first step is to ask what kind of question is being raised. Questions can usually be placed in one of two categories: answerable and unanswerable. By answerable we mean questions for which there is available observable evidence to support an answer. The questions may not be easy, and considerable effort and persistence may be necessary to arrive at an answer, but these questions can usually be identified as answerable. Unanswerable questions, on the other hand, lack what is usually referred to as observable sensory information, referred to as empirical evidence. This does not mean that answers are not suggested, it just means that the answers are expressed more as hopes, speculation, or matters of faith. The basis for answers changes, and that's where things become controversial. Questions of this sort might be referred to as timeless questions growing out of the mysteries of life.

Questions Arising from the Cause of Death

To provide an illustration of answerable questions, we review the questions that often arise around the various causes of death. These can be troublesome and disturbing questions, and finding answers may be difficult, but they are the kinds of questions that most likely have answers. They are provided here as illustrations.

Natural Causes. Was this really a natural cause or an unidentified but treatable illness? At what age does a patient's illness and death become natural? Why is the cause of this death called natural, even though it was rare and unexpected? Why did the person die of this disease or condition instead of recovering from it?

Disruptive Illness. Why would a person in otherwise good health contract this illness or condition? Is disease leading to death explainable or merely random? Why did this happen at this point in this person's life? Could this illness have been prevented or another treatment provided? Why was the recovery only temporary?

Accident. What steps could have been taken to prevent this death? Why did it occur at this particular time and place? Was there negligence? Is someone responsible? Should legal action be taken?

Natural Disaster. Why did this disastrous event take place at precisely this location and at this exact time? Were the response time and method of responding sufficient? Why were lives lost instead of saved? Was there an adequate warning? Could those who died have been evacuated to somewhere else on time?

Homicide. Who did this and what was the motive? Was this a planned homicide or a random act of violence? Can anything be done to control and prevent random homicide?

Military. How did diplomacy in this instance fail to produce peace? Why was this person deployed at this time and place and how did they become the one to die when others survived? Were these military operations necessary for the defense of the country?

Suicide. Should this be identified as a suicide or a drug overdose? Was the death accidental or truly intentional? How did things get so bad that the person wanted to take their own life? Did they leave a note for survivors to explain what they were going through? Who is responsible and to what extent? Why wasn't this death prevented?

It is tempting to dismiss these questions by stating that they can't be answered, but these questions are clearly legitimate and deserve thoughtful consideration. This is especially true where responsibility is unclear and needs to be established. Most of the questions associated with the manner of death do have answers. Sometimes the pursuit of these questions interferes with or delays the tasks of mourning, but many of these questions deserve priority and "due diligence" in pursuit of answers.

When someone dies, numerous questions spring up. In this first flurry of questions there is often a mingling of questions that appear not to have answers with questions that have answers, or at least could have answers, if vigorously and responsibly pursued. An initial task confronting the mourner is to sort out questions that can and should be answered from those that are likely unanswerable, those larger philosophical questions that most likely do not have answers based on empirical evidence.

DIALOGUE

Mourner: When my first wife died unexpectedly in the middle of the night, surprising us all and leaving us so suddenly, her family—mother, brother, sisters—wanted to know what happened. Not that they were suspicious, they just wanted to understand, and so did my daughters and I.

Counselor: A reasonable concern. And how did you get answers?

Mourner: We arranged for an autopsy and the report was prompt and revealing. Perhaps the doctors had a better understanding of her condition, but we certainly didn't know how developed her cancer was. The report showed that the lymphoma had spread to several parts of her body, including a shoulder bone and her heart, but the cause of death was a cancer-induced abscess that had developed on the intestine and burst the peritoneum, the membrane lining the abdomen. That's what happened on that fatal night.

Counselor: And how did you feel when you finally learned that?

Mourner: Relieved to know and glad that we had an explanation. After learning that her cancer had come back, weeks before her death, my wife wanted to know why she had terminal cancer. I will never forget the night when her oncologist came into the hospital room at the end of his rounds, took off his white coat, and sat in the chair beside her bed, ready to listen. She unleashed a flood of questions, mostly concerning how this type of cancer could come to such a young and otherwise healthy person. Was she to blame for something? After listening carefully, the doctor responded, "I have come to realize after years of practicing medicine that some things are just random." It was a good scientist's answer to a question with no immediate scientific answer. Some things just happen without explanation. It was a relief for her to hear, especially after her friends at that time were providing her with so many ridiculous explanations for her condition. No, it wasn't anything she was or was not doing.

Counselor: It must have been liberating for her to know she was not responsible.

Mourner: For sure. Our handicapped daughter, who died many years later was not a healthy person, and perhaps we should have raised more questions about her diet and sedentary life in assisted living.

Counselor: I suppose you could have pursued those questions, but again, those features of her lifestyle may not have been to blame. "Randomness" could have applied to her as well.

Mourner: Yes, those aspects of her later life go hand in hand with confinement to a wheelchair in an institutional setting, but I have always wondered why it was ovarian cancer that caused her death. She had had an early hysterectomy, but apparently it was the practice to let the ovaries remain under those circumstances for the purpose of hormone balance. Then, ironically, that's what caused her death, ovarian cancer.

Counselor: Yes, probably a standard protocol under the circumstances, but hindsight carries a different perspective. You are not alone having these questions about "what if it had been done differently," and "could this fateful outcome have been avoided?" Do questions like this come to mind about your other losses?

Mourner: Oh, yes. Let me tell you the story about my brother. It's got some questions. He lived in a small town surrounded by other nearby towns, and as a bit of a hypochondriac he visited many doctors without any real coordination among them on medication. At one point he was taking twenty-four pills a day. So first of all, how was that allowed to happen? He was ill and got a lot worse, and when the hospital sent him to hospice to die, the hospice, as is the practice, took all his meds away. And guess what, he got better.

Counselor: Really? What happened?

Mourner: He got so much better they had to release him from hospice care. The president of the college where he served came to visit him, and so my brother told him he was graduating—from hospice. "Graduating?' the president asked skeptically. "No, my friend," he said, "I think you flunked out."

Counselor: Flunked out of hospice? Oh, that's a good one. What happened to him?

Mourner: He lived for two more years and eventually died of a heart condition at home. But think of the questions. Why did the hospital send him to hospice care? Was it really time to do that? Was he cured by accident? What if they had taken away a crucial medication and he died prematurely because of it? In his case, the questions were real and answerable, but we didn't pursue them because he got better. I wish sometimes that I had asked more questions about my daughter, too, before she fell into such suffering.

Counselor: It seems like when someone dies, it is natural for a lot of questions to surface about the circumstances.

The Existential Quest for Meaning

When the important, answerable questions have been identified and pursued diligently, the mourner is still left with a host of questions that appear to have no answers. Some people might ask: If they have no answers, then why pursue them? Because unanswered questions will pursue the mourner, sometimes relentlessly. In some situations, unanswered questions can contribute to mental or physical distress, whirling around in the mind without resolution. The task, then, is not so much to find answers, but to provide a framework for exploring and living with disturbing questions, as part of the broader process of adapting to loss. It helps to learn what others think about these questions.

The challenge of adapting to the flood of deeper questions that come with loss is what J. William Worden refers to as "the existential quest for meaning." (Worden, 2019, p. 189) This quest for meaning contains personal questions relating to the very foundations of one's existence. Worden notes that when a loss has occurred, those who survive not only ask "why this has happened, but also why did this happen to me? (Worden, 2018, p. 101)

To these basic questions we add a list of additional questions in Figure 11 to elaborate the concept of the existential quest for meaning.

Figure 11

List of Existential Questions

Why are we born?

Where do we come from?

Do we have a personal destiny?

Can we choose what happens to us?

Do we have a soul?

Is there a possibility of life after death?

Is rebirth an option?

What is our place in the universe?

Why must living things die?

Is there any ultimate meaning to life?

If life is without purpose, is it possible to create purpose?

What is a good life?

These are questions that a person from any culture might ask at any stage of life, and while many people conscientiously pursue answers, others do not, choosing instead to ignore, avoid, or repress such difficult questions. But when a loss occurs, existential questions seem to pop up dramatically and demand attention, adding more work to the already difficult process of grieving.

We refer to these questions as the timeless questions that grow out of the mysteries of life. Each of the questions listed in Figure 11 appears to be grounded in some deep, unsolved mystery involving the nature and meaning of human existence. They are "timeless" questions because generation after generation of human beings keeps asking them. This is not so much because the answers are poor, but because the questions cannot be answered easily or satisfactorily. So, people continue to ask them and have for thousands of years because life is filled with mystery.

It is not surprising that books on grief seldom address these questions. Certainly, no author is to be blamed for this omission. Exploring these questions involves stepping outside of the presumed expertise of the social sciences and treading on the turf of other fields in the humanities, particularly in philosophy, literature, and religious studies. The discussion gets very complicated rather quickly with differing views of what constitutes scholarship and evidence. Providers of help may not feel comfortable with these questions, and the temptation is to avoid such discussions. But people who suffer loss *have* these existential questions and usually want to explore them. We venture cautiously into this domain by providing an interdisciplinary perspective on these questions.

RELIGIOUS TRADITIONS AND TIMELESS QUESTIONS

Perhaps the only subject with a greater taboo than death and grief is the ultra-taboo subject of religion. People are reluctant to discuss religion because they are uncomfortable with the subject and don't want to offend anyone by saying the wrong thing. But religion is also a field of study, and people vary widely in their understanding of it, not only what they think, but how they think about it. Sometimes they hold very strong beliefs, beliefs mixed with doubts, or no beliefs at all. For that reason, serious discussion of religion seems to be shrouded in respectful silence.

The world's religious traditions, particularly in their ancient and original form, have had many things to say about the timeless questions and mysteries of life. One might even suggest a hypothesis, as we do here, that timeless questions based on the mysteries of life are what give rise to religion. Religious traditions formulate and frame the questions as well as suggest options and answers. Some people like the answers and become followers of a particular faith, others are not so sure and keep looking, still others are sure this is not the place to look. In the remainder of this lesson, we explore what some of the major world religions have had to say about three questions that are often in the minds of mourners: Is there life after death? What is the meaning of life? What is a good life?

Before embarking on that journey, it may be useful to explore briefly what is meant by religious belief and whether it is even possible in today's post-Enlightenment world. The modern issues of belief are set forth with amazing clarity in a classic essay entitled "The Will to Believe" by William James, 1842–1910, a Harvard professor at the time who later came to be known as the founder of the field called "the psychology of religion." He is best known for his book, *The Varieties of Religious Experience*.

As James points out, our rational nature and respect for the rules of science make belief very difficult for the modern individual. We have been taught to respect and look for objective and observable evidence, but as James notes, in religious beliefs, such as a belief in a force beyond the visible world, the "much lauded objective evidence is never triumphantly there." How could there be objective certitude about something that is beyond empirical observation? A religious belief, James suggests, might be set up as a hypothesis to be weighed, with the hope of finding truth.

For William James, believing involves aspects of the self, such as feelings and intuition; and the rational self, while not to be discarded, is not the only consideration. He quotes Pascal, but it is a line that goes back to Shakespeare, "The heart has its reasons of which reason has no knowledge." Thus, James expands on the conception of self as going beyond the observing and reasoning self of science, suggesting that there is more to belief than reason, and more to religious belief than objective evidence and certainty. It seems then, for James, that in matters of the heart there is no proof "beyond a reasonable doubt" either for or against belief, and he finds it okay to "adopt a believing attitude" based on an expanded view of the self, as a person trying to make conscientious choices about beliefs. (James in Pelikan, 1990, pp. 95-114) Incidentally, psychology of religion, the field that James founded, explores the effects of religious belief, not the truth of its propositions, as a way to learn more about how belief affects behavior.

The reason for exploring this essay by James is not to enlist belief but to use if for thinking about what belief might be. It provides a framework for understanding the wide spectrum of belief and unbelief that exists, not only in those who grieve but in their helpers. As each individual approaches timeless questions, there will be some who expect conclusive objective evidence and want nothing to do with religious belief. There will be some who sense the limits of science and regard the imposing of scientific method onto every type of question as "scientism." There are some who wish to broaden the concept of self to incorporate belief but can't quite part with their rational outlook. Others will have strong traditional beliefs and little concern about evidence as the basis of their faith. Among those who believe, there will be those who take their foundational scriptures very literally and others who understand them metaphorically as an illuminating story or myth. It is important to learn about and understand these differences and where people stand along the spectrum of belief. Keeping these differences in mind, it is possible now to explore what classical world religious traditions have had to say about the three selected questions and how these may (or may not) be helpful to the mourner's existential quest for meaning.

In what follows, we have drawn extensively and freely without specific references to a book about world religions by one of the authors. (Davis, 2022) See the Annotated Bibliography for more information about that work.

Life After Death

One of the first questions for mourners on their quest for existential meaning has to do with what happens, if anything, to the deceased. The famous poet Alfred Lord Tennyson, 1809–1892, expresses this boldly in these lines from *Maud,* cited in Moffat, 1992, p. 171.

> Ah Christ! That it were possible
> For one short hour to see
> The souls we loved, that they might tell us
> What and where they be.

Yes, both what and where. What form do they take and where are they? Those are questions commonly raised by those who mourn.

The rational and scientific perspective is that, as far as we know, when a person dies, their brain no longer functions. It is as if they are sleeping and don't awaken, and because they don't wake up, they don't know that they didn't wake up. They are now in a state of non-being. That is the end, a rationalist would say, and let's just leave it at that. Some people can accept that explanation as final and complete, but many people throughout the world and across the centuries have sought other explanations that elaborate the what and where of life beyond death. Whether one believes these explanations or not, it is useful to know about them.

Popular culture is filled with ideas about life after death floating around unattached to any tradition of origin. Heaven is up; hell is down. Heaven has pearly gates and an attendant monitoring entry. The "soul" leaves the body behind and floats up to heaven. Some get in, some don't. It may be necessary to wait until judgment day to find out. Similarly, there are popular ideas about reincarnation where the soul leaves for a brief stay somewhere before returning to a new life on earth. Another popular idea is that the elements of the body become reunited somehow with the elements of the universe, and not just in the grave. Some people will be caught up in these popular ideas and may be less familiar with concepts grounded in historical religious traditions. Others may have grown up in a religious tradition against which they have rebelled or which they have modified and still find meaningful.

As an example of traditional belief, reincarnation, or more accurately, rebirth, has ancient roots in Hinduism, a religion of the original people of India. Hinduism has many gods (known as polytheism), but also has the larger unifying concept of *brahman,* the deeper spiritual reality that pervades the universe, and *atman,* the sacred self that dwells within all persons.

Basic to the idea of rebirth is the concept of *karma,* a word that has become popular in the West, suggesting that every human action has good or bad consequences that accumulate, not only in this life, but beyond in future lives. Karma might be thought of as a built-in accounting system for what people do, so the goal is to add good deeds and avoid bad karma. At death, a person will be reborn, either moving upward in human existence, or backward into non-human forms of life. The ultimate goal within Hinduism is to arrive at *moksha,* a state of liberation from the process of rebirth and to enter into God-realization, a state of closeness to God.

Rebirth, as one view of life after death, speaks to the timeless questions of what happens and where. It also addresses other issues, such as disparities of advantage or disadvantage at the time of birth, and the issue of justice for the bad things that happen to good people. It also provides another chance for finishing the unfinished work of life. Many Hindus hold some form of belief in rebirth, and the ideas of "reincarnation" and "karma" are sometimes popular today among those who don't regard themselves as Hindu.

Buddhism, having historical roots in Hinduism, took another path under the guidance of Siddhartha Gautama, c. 485–410 or 400 BCE, who came to be known as Buddha. The idea of escaping rebirth, the cycle of *samsara*, is a more intense concern in Buddhism because of its heightened perception of the degree of suffering built into life in this world. A respectful, but humorous characterization, of the Buddhist view of life might be "Let me out of here."

Relieving suffering, both physical and emotional, by letting go of personal attachments to things and people, is an important part of Buddhist Enlightenment, but so is caring for others who suffer. In fact, those who truly follow the teachings and emulate the caring life of Buddha may come back to life after death as *bodhisattvas,* human incarnations of the earthly Buddha, avatars destined to return to life to relieve the suffering of others. For Buddhism, in thinking about an afterlife, the focus is on Enlightenment, a process that includes meditation and mindfulness and is built upon inner peace and gradual spiritual detachment from the self.

Although Buddhism does not have much to say about a god of creation, there is a complex cosmology of spheres, realms, and eons, designating vast space and thousands of years of time. In Buddhism, life is played out on a gigantic stage with plenty of room for those who come before and those who come after, giving magnified cosmic importance to human life in a spacious cosmos. Buddhism, then, also speaks to the timeless question about the what and where of life after death, but it puts more emphasis on human suffering and the need to break the continuous circle of recycled life, and doing so through Enlightenment.

Islam developed somewhat later than most of the historic faiths, beginning, according to tradition, with the first words of Allah to the Prophet Mohammed in 610 CE. Drawing on the earlier monotheistic traditions of Judaism and Christianity, Islam has a strong concept of the return of the individual at death to Allah. Muslim monotheism means more than belief in One God; it is the God of Oneness who unifies everything. It is natural, then, to think of a reunion with God at death, since nothing exists apart from God, there being no division between this world and the hereafter. There is a concept of Paradise in Islam, described in the Quran with clear images of flowing streams, people sitting in the shade of palm trees, and neither extremes of heat nor cold. These components of paradise are things not automatically available in the lands of Arabia. The what and where of a continuing existence is in a pleasant paradise, and with reunification with the God of Oneness.

Christianity developed a strong concept of the afterlife based on the belief in the resurrection of Jesus, although there is not much about an afterlife in the teachings of Jesus recorded in the Gospels. The Greek concept of a soul, freed from the body, was widespread at the time, and still is today in popular culture, but the traditional Christian view, often confused with the Greek, is not about the release of the soul, but the resurrection of the body. The idea is recited in the Apostles Creed as "the resurrection of the body and the life everlasting." This is not the body people have when they die, but a new body and soul—body, psyche, spirit, mind—integrated and restored in a new being, capable of living a new but continuing life. Death, in the Christian tradition can be viewed, not so much as a destruction of the body to free the soul, but as a metamorphosis into a new being with a more complete relationship with God. The question about what place and form life takes after death is expressed as transformation into a new being close to God.

Other religious traditions, surprisingly, don't have much to say about life after death. Confucianism, growing out of the philosophy of Confucius, 551–479 BCE, doesn't offer much, as if the subject were put to rest by his saying, "You don't understand life, how can you understand death?" Another major religious tradition of East Asia identified as Taoism, places emphasis on longevity and living a simple life, suggesting only vaguely that at death there will probably be some kind of transformation.

The point of this exploration is not to advocate or criticize any particular view of life after death, but to provide background and illustrations of options that may come up for contemplation and discussion. These are ideas that are "out there," and most mourners know about them and will want and need to talk about them, sometimes as beliefs or simply as dreams, longings, and hopes. Although the afterlife is a controversial issue, it is a prominent issue for many who grieve, and diverse options may be strongly denied or sympathetically embraced.

Consider the following two quotations. First, the well-known fiction author Pearl Buck, 1892–1973, in pondering the possibility of a life beyond, wrote these words, as cited in Moffat, 1992, p.220.

I remembered the courage of his atheism.

She is expressing the view that it took courage not to believe. The timeless questions are so urgent, so puzzling, so in need of answers, that it takes courage, she suggests, not to provide them. In the second quote, at the other extreme, is an expression of faith so strong, so filled with conviction, and so lacking in doubt, that the expression of it becomes almost humorous. The passage is by the beloved African American author, Alice Walker, born in1944, from *Goodnight, Willie Lee,* as cited in Moffat, 1992, p.160.

Looking down into my father's
dead face
for the last time
my mother said without
tears, without smiles,
without regrets
but with *civility*
"Good night, Willie Lee, I'll see you
In the morning."

These are some of the ways that thoughtful people of differing cultures and traditions have learned to adapt to persistent timeless questions about life after death.

Most religions not only have beliefs, but practices and active observances that come from beliefs. The psychologist Ruth Malkinson, writing in *Cognitive Grief Therapy*, identifies certain of these structured practices as "leave-taking rituals," meaning the things that are done in a particular tradition to help the mourner separate from the deceased, as they are dying or after death, or to wish them well on their journey into another life. (Malkinson, 2007, p. 161) As the major religious traditions have developed over time, so have their mourning practices to the point that it is difficult to single out patterns as being typical. It is possible, however, to provide examples of what people do as they encounter the mystery of death and express what they feel they need to do to say good-bye. The authors of selected chapters in Colin Parkes stimulating book, *Death and Bereavement Across Cultures*, provide the accounts summarized here. (Parkes, 2015)

HINDU LEAVE-TAKING RITUAL

In an upper caste Hindu family, a male spouse, the head of the family, is surrounded by friends and other family members as he dies in the hospital at age 72. When the eldest son, now in charge, pays the bills, a death certificate is provided, and the body is sent by ambulance to the family home. The body, when it arrives, is taken to the bedroom of the deceased and placed, not on the bed, but on the floor, as is the custom. The sons draft an obituary, notify friends and the rest of the family, as cooks and cleaners are hired for a twelve-day ceremony at home. Priests are invited into the house, and they read from sacred texts and recite holy verses from the Gita while also singing devotional songs. The family priest from the local temple is also summoned. Friends and neighbors participate in daily prayer meetings at sunrise and sunset. The sons go to the garden to have their hair cut off and their heads shaved. The courtyard is turned into a kitchen to prepare food for numerous guests. Upstairs, mourners assemble and sit cross-legged on the floor near the body to engage in silent prayers. Other guests arrive from India and distant places.

Later, the sons wash their father's body and prepare it for the funeral. They wrap the body in muslin, place it on a movable platform (a bier) and bring it downstairs as the crowd watches, chanting and weeping. The priest heads the funeral procession to the crematorium. The body is now in a coffin, as it is carried the long distance there by the brothers. The body is eventually placed in one of the six burning ghats with its pyre of stacked logs. After prayers in Sanskrit by the priest, the eldest son is handed a torch to light the pyre. Guests remain in a separate room or are free to leave. Later, an attendant collects ashes in an urn for the eldest son. The ashes will eventually be immersed in the Ganges River. For the remainder of the twelve days, guests continue to visit the home and the priest offers prayers, readings, and songs from the Hindu religious tradition. (Pittu and Ann Laungani in Parkes, et.al., 2015, Chapter 4, pp.42-60)

BUDDHIST LEAVE-TAKING RITUAL

For this follower of Buddha, a calm and quiet deathbed is provided so that the individual can have a proper frame of mind to focus on the Dharma (teachings) and prepare for the next rebirth. One who dies in an agitated state may have more difficulty finding a good rebirth. Thus, there is in Buddhist tradition, a strong focus on providing a peaceful death, taking refuge in calm, holding beads or sacred objects, and listening to recordings of chants. Sudden death or commotion associated with injury is dreaded. After death, the body is not touched or moved until it has cooled, a period of around six hours. Funerals vary but include chants and readings of sacred texts dedicated to the deceased. Buddhist practices permit all manner of bodily disposal: burial, immersion in water, cremation, and exposure to air. There is a preference to keep observances simple and humble. Memorials may be held after seven days, three months, and as an anniversary on the date of the death for ten years. Remembrance days may include flowers, photographs, or money-raising memorials. Mourners eat a vegetarian diet and avoid alcohol for forty-nine days, at which point they feel assured that the deceased has acquired a new life. (Gouin Margareb in Parkes, 2015, pp. 61-75)

ISLAMIC LEAVE-TAKING RITUAL

The goal through illness is healing, if possible, to restore the person as a being made in the image of God and to relieve suffering as much as possible. Life is a journey and when a person dies, they begin a journey to eternal life. Death is regarded as the Will of Allah and as with all else in life involves submission to that Will. Allah is not the name of God, but refers to Al Lah, meaning *The God*. The Quran teaches that "No soul knows the exact time of his death." The human journey is summarized as "We came from Allah and unto Him is our return." The prophet Mohammed is reported to have said, "Man is asleep and when he dies, he wakes up." Thus, the belief in life after death in Islam is strong and certain. A modest funeral is held, led by an Imam asking Allah for forgiveness and blessings. Only men attend the burial. There are no wreaths or flowers, just prayers for the deceased and other souls buried in the cemetery. The soul returns to God. A mourning period is usually restricted to three days. (Waseem Alladin in Parkes, 2015, pp.110-132)

OTHER MOURNING PRACTICES

George Bonanno identifies other mourning practices that reverse the focus of leave-taking, where the usual focus is on the mourner, to draw attention to the journey of the person who has died. In traditional Chinese rituals, the goal is to help the deceased make their way to the land of the dead and find a good life there. In Taiwan, ceremonies of several hours include an arranged trip to visit the dead to check on loved ones. In Mexico, the dead are invited back to earth to visit the living in a national observance known as The Day of the Dead. A particular day is set aside to prepare beautiful but modest altars of remembrance, inviting the deceased to return for a visit, a practice thought to be an ancient custom that preceded the arrival of the Spanish. People of West Africa in the Republic of Benin even hold a parade of costumed villagers and tell humorous stories to welcome back the dead in a communal observance. (Bonanno, 2019, pp. 242, 236, 238)

In the aboriginal traditions of the North-west Coast Cultures (Native American in the U.S. and First Nation Peoples in Canada), intermingling with the deceased includes animal as well as human spirits where humans can flow into other forms, be taken prisoner temporarily by animal spirits, and eventually return to human society. These transformations are symbolized in the mixing of human and animal forms in artistic creations and masks that suggest another being behind the mask. (Geertz in Hinnels, 2010, p. 524) Southwest Pueblo cultures in the U.S. hold elaborate Kachina ceremonies where ancestral spirits—human, animal, and superhuman— arrive and depart with seasonal fluctuations. (Geertz in Hinnels, 2010, pp.540-541) The Ute Indians, living in what became

Colorado and Utah, were sincere believers in immortality, and after a battle between an evil spirit and a good spirit for the soul of the deceased, usually won by the good spirit, the Indian's soul was conducted to the Happy Hunting Ground. (Rockwell, 2006, p.46)

The human imagination, over many centuries, seems to have no limits in designing rituals and practices to assist the mourner in taking leave from the dead, to help the dead leave on their journey to an afterlife, to find ways for mourners to go check on the deceased, and to get everybody back together again on earth for special days of remembrance. The mysteries associated with death and the fate of those who die are so great, that humans find it difficult to live without explanations. The content and beliefs supported by specific rituals may not be as important as the intensity of the experience that generates them. The search for explanations, any plausible and comforting explanation, is persistent, widespread, and unending in human cultures over time.

Most people will have some established idea about what they believe or do not believe about life after death, and their beliefs and doubts will influence how they go about mourning and leave-taking practices. On the other hand, the emotional shock and disruption of thinking patterns in grief may create the need for some reconsideration or reconstruction of views about life after death. It is natural at this time of loss to want to reexamine old beliefs and consider new ones, to rethink doubts or become more certain about them. Some mourners may be discussing these issues for the first time ever; for others it may have been many years since they have had such discussions. Those with traditional beliefs but shattered hearts may be seeking reassurance. What is needed is a very safe space characterized by openness and tolerance for those seeking serious discussion. Others may prefer the solitude of a quiet corner for resolving by themselves as best they can the mysteries associated with death.

THE MEANING OF LIFE

The loss of a person to death is sometimes accompanied by a loss of meaning, the feeling that one's own personal life isn't worth living any more, but also by a broader existential outlook that life in general is meaningless. Mourners will comment frequently on feeling lost, without purpose, without much enthusiasm for living. The famous playwright and poet William Shakespeare, 1564–1616, provides words for that loss of motivation in *Hamlet,* Act I, Scene 2, as cited in Moffat, 1992, p. 55.

> How weary, stale, flat and
>   unprofitable,
> Seem to me all the uses of
>   this world.

Many of the things that one enjoyed in life before the loss—work, conversation, home, hobbies, relationships, entertainment—are not as they once were. Something is missing. Yes, of course, it is the deceased, but with that loss comes a broader deprivation, a sense that now a presence that once animated life and made each day worth living, is absent. To borrow Shakespeare's words: "weary," meaning tired out, without energy or motivation; "stale," meaning nothing new or fresh, just repetitive and unimaginative; "flat," meaning without variation, tedious, monotonous, and boring; and "unprofitable," meaning pointless. Life like this becomes life not worth living.

Megan DeVine once again rescues the mourner with these insightful words of wisdom: "Not wanting to be alive is not the same thing as wanting to be dead." (DeVine, 2017, p. 102) A person with true suicidal thoughts, including how to go about it, needs immediate help, but the typical "resilient' mourner can have normal feelings about how difficult it is to be alive, without wanting to be dead. The challenge is to find ways to transform a "weary, stale, flat and unprofitable" life into one that once again has purpose, vibrance, motivation, and meaning.

The grief specialist and thanatologist (one who studies death), David Kessler, provides his thoughts on this in his book *Finding Meaning.* (Kessler, 2019) We have brought together his suggestions in a summary and interpretation. Naturally, as with other aspects of grief, the need varies with kinship and manner of death, the extent of the shattering of meaning, and the resources survivors have available to recover it. Although many aspects of what happened are beyond the mourner's power to change, Kessler points out that "We *do* have power to change our thoughts," adding, "Whatever thoughts you water are the thoughts that will grow." (Kessler, 2019, p. 73) In other words, mental attitude is important in restoring meaning and "the story you tell yourself repeatedly becomes your meaning." It is as if we write the script and then act the part, so it is tempting to take on the role of victim, continuing to ask repeatedly, Why me?

It is not easy to get beyond the images of failure associated with dying—heart failure, kidney failure, succumbed, lost the battle, or didn't make it—but in the end we all "fail." Death appears to triumph, and we all seem to lose. But Kessler notes that "the way we view death, reflects how we look at life." What we need is a more positive view of both, and to find ways to regain meaning. (Kessler, 2019, p. 71, p. 55)

A central theme of Kessler's suggestions is to memorialize the deceased in some way, to get beyond passive self-preoccupying misery, and to get up and do something significant on behalf of the deceased. This includes not only the standard memorials associated with mourning but living in such a way as to acknowledge meaning in how the deceased lived. Kessler suggests that mourners might ask, "What did your loved one get out of being here? And what did you get out of knowing him or her? (Kessler, 2019, p.99) In making meaning, the task is to bring forth something good from this death.

Beyond physical memorials one might consider the identification and support of a significant cause. But there is also the more modest task of "finding a connection with that person that you carry forward into your own life." (Kessler, 2019, p.211) In that way, survivors become the legacy of the deceased. It's a choice: to remain a victim or become the creator of a new legacy of meaning for the one you loved.

Although these suggestions may not work for everyone or in every circumstance of death, the idea of making meaning out of the loss itself is challenging but creative. We might say, however, that these are ideas about making meaning in the sense of a lower case "m," the meaning that animates the living of daily life. Lurking around the corner are the concerns about capital "M" meaning, the questions about whether life in general has meaning or is simply pointless and absurd.

In general, the religious traditions speak to the capital "M" question of meaning through their ideas about God, creation, and the good life. There seems to be agreement within them, though not uniform belief, that human life has a God-given meaning, that God brings individuals from non-being into being, and that beliefs about life after death assume that life before death is of such value that it is worth continuing.

On the other hand, some would say that the ancient religious traditions are just that: ancient and outdated, and that we now live in a God-is-dead world in which each individual is trying to make sense of human existence independently. Naturally, those who grieve will be spread over this wide spectrum of belief and non-belief, but the continuum may include significant numbers of mourners who, because of their loss, are having a crisis of belief and a diminished sense of the meaning of life in general. If encouraged, they may wish to think through their crumbling sense of the meaning of life. Can this be discussed outside of religious faith?

The topic of meaning has been addressed at length by Albert Camus, a Frenchman (actually Algerian), quoted earlier, writing at the time of World War II and after. As both a philosopher and novelist, what he seemed to be saying was that life is not only meaningless and pointless in a neutral sense, but actually absurd, meaning ridiculous, crazy, stupid, and preposterous. Yes, as in, Isn't life absurd? In his writing, Camus sticks to his atheist views and insists that we accept the absurdity of this closed universe. Instead of belief in a Divine Being, or even a reasonable universe, Camus suggests that if we truly embrace absurdity, we will want to rebel against it and fight back, a view elaborated in his philosophical book, *The Rebel*. Then Camus goes a step farther in a novel he calls *The Plague*. In the story, the plague has aspects of the bubonic plague, complete with rats, but the plague is much more than that, perhaps a symbol of all of the absurdities of life. The main character, Doctor Rieux, fights the plague—that is his mission in life—and he does so without understanding exactly how to fight it and without knowing if he will succeed or die in the process. He just knows that he must resist, rebel, and fight against absurdity on behalf of humanity. In life, Camus acted upon what he taught: he was an underground French resistance fighter in World War II. The message is that one creates meaning in life by trying to do some good in the fight against absurdity.

Finding meaning and Meaning are often challenges to those who mourn, as these difficult questions are aggravated by loss. Adapting to the timeless question about meaning may also be thought of as another challenge of mourning.

The Good Life

If the resilient mourner is able to explore and resolve to some extent the puzzling questions about life after death, and then restore meaning to a shattered life, one more challenge awaits. What if the goal is not only to adapt, endure, and "set out again," but to learn from loss how to live a better life. Is this asking too much of those who painfully grieve? To set out again without the deceased and try to live a better life? But what is meant by better? Better than what? How could one still struggling with the sadness of loss take on that challenge?

People think of many diverse ways to lead their lives. Some focus on work, choosing either the branching path to financial success or career satisfaction, sometimes both. Others choose family, where having and raising children becomes the consuming task or source of satisfaction. Others turn a hobby or sport into nearly a career, drawing more satisfaction from it than work or family and turning it into a way to measure accomplishment. Some devote themselves to music or the arts, drawing enjoyment from aesthetic activity while others seek out nature and find enjoyment outdoors. Some make a life out of reading or writing. Two questions arise. What is the good life? Is it possible to find it, choose it, and live it?

The famous author and naturalist Henry David Thoreau went out to nearby Walden Pond seeking the good life. He noticed a lot of conformity in the lives of his neighbors, people doing what everyone else does without much thought as to why they are doing it. It inspired the sentence, "The mass of men" (and women) "lead lives of quiet desperation." What Thoreau meant by that is that few people actually chose to lead the life they are living. They seem to be just going through the motions. Here, in his own words, from *Walden,* first published in 1854, is Thoreau's reason for going to Walden Pond. (Thoreau, 1982, p.172)

> I went to the woods because I wished to live
> deliberately, to front only the essential facts of life,
> and see if I could not learn what it had to teach, and
> not, when I came to die, discover that I had not lived.

Thoreau's words "live deliberately" suggest a choice, as opposed to chance, habit, or routine. Some mourners don't have much choice; they must face the responsibilities they have, sometimes filled with a sense of panic. But for many mourners, the death of a loved one becomes a choice point. What do I do now? Options open. Thoreau wanted to be deliberate, but he also hoped to find out what the good life is, and to live it, so that when he died, he wouldn't wonder if he had missed the point of life. Sometimes those who mourn will want to re-examine their entire life and may feel the need to reflect on their options for moving forward.

The religious traditions, each in their own way, have had things to say about the good life. Hinduism breaks life into stages, and the good life is different, depending on whether a person is a student, a householder, a forest dweller, or hermit, with the highest goal being to understand one's soul (atman) and to draw closer to ultimate reality (brahman). Integral to the good life is yoga, which is not just a set of stretching exercises, but a means of linking (the word *yoga* means yoke) with the God Ishvara through mental communication. Yoga is often thought of as static meditation, but among four types of yoga is Karma yoga, which moves the person beyond contemplation to action, useful and unselfish work, spontaneous good deeds.

Siddhartha led a sheltered life as a child and young man, but one day he travelled by chariot outside of his father's estate and encountered old age, sickness, and death. It shocked him and set off a search for the good life that led to his recognition as the Buddha. Siddhartha experimented with many ways of living and eventually chose a path toward Enlightenment that included not only a calm mind and serene manner, but also serious efforts to contain and relieve suffering, one's own and that of others, as the key to the good life. Buddhism developed the *sangha*, a monastic community, and a wanderer's way of life, and later a path to Enlightenment for people who lived an everyday life. But whatever the way, a person needs to work at the good life to find Enlightenment.

Confucius, 551–479 BCE, taught filial piety as respect for and reverence for one's parents as the beginning of the good life, but he is most remembered for his teaching about social structure and good government. The good life was based on the simple moral virtue of acknowledging one's humanity linked to the humanity of others. Confucius saw the good life as walking in another person's shoes.

In a similar way, the Jewish tradition in the Hebrew Scriptures places a strong emphasis on the communal life of a people, one might say good lives, in the plural. Surely the message of the prophets is filled with concern for "social justice" well summarized in the words of the prophet Micah: "He has showed you, O, Man, what is good; and what does the Lord require of you but to do justice, and to love kindness, and to walk humbly with your God? (Micah 6:8)

The Christian idea of the good life is based not so much on good deeds that become a path to salvation, as the recognition that one is already forgiven and loved unconditionally by God. The good life involves responding to that redemption in a like manner by leading a forgiving and loving life.

Sometimes people within historical religious traditions live not only a good life, but a truly outstanding life. Bodhisattvas come to mind in Buddhism, people who have done so much good in life that they are brought back to do more. Exceptionally good people within Catholic Christianity are sometimes canonized as Saints. Perhaps the most familiar Saint is Mother Thresa, who began her work as a nun of the Sisters of Loreto, working on the streets of Calcutta, India, generating food and medical services for the impoverished, sick, and dying. At the time of her death, she had founded her own Order, with nearly 4,000 Missions of Charity in 120 countries, having been awarded a Nobel Prize for her compassionate service to the poor. And then, designated Sainthood.

The Protestant churches don't have a formal system for canonizing saints, but they do have outstanding people who lead extraordinary lives. A good example is Albert Schweitzer, who was known not only for his critical studies of the New Testament, but as a renowned scholar of the composer Bach and an accomplished organist who also knew how to repair pipe organs. He is best known, however, for his missionary work as "Jungle Doctor" in Africa, a caring physician who was also competent in raising money for his causes. His careers went on for many years in diverse and creative directions. One might think that such a person would have a complex view of life, but Schweitzer is also known, perhaps even best known, for his simple philosophy of Reverence for Life, simply giving respect to every living thing in its struggle to live. The good life doesn't get much plainer than that.

It is tempting to dismiss the good life of these individuals as being beyond the reach of the ordinary person, not something that can be achieved. But it is important to remember that these *were* ordinary people, of humble origins, and what they did was difficult for them as it would be for anyone to achieve. It required enormous effort. The goal, of course, is not necessarily to become a Saint, but for each mourner to use the occasion of mourning to contemplate the good life, to make deliberate choices, and to learn new things in the process about one's interests, commitments, and capabilities.

A FINAL LESSON FOR LEARNING FROM LOSS

This Fifth Lesson for Learning from Loss has explored with interdisciplinary perspectives some of the existential questions that frequently arise from the experience of the death of a loved one. Many of these are "timeless questions" that have no conclusive answers. Not all of the questions on the list provided have been addressed, but three have been explored in some detail, mostly as illustrations of how to begin to think about them. These include questions about Life After Death, The Meaning of Life, and the Good Life.

Mourners vary considerably in what they believe about these questions, how they think about belief, and how they devise tentative answers with or without religious belief. We recognize that some mourners will find these questions more important than others. Some may have little patience for them in the difficult present moments of their grief. Some may not have the luxury of time or energy to explore them, and others may not feel comfortable enough to break the taboo about discussing them. Our working hypothesis has been that at some point these questions will arise, perhaps very forcefully, and in a variety of forms, for those who experience loss through death. Addressing these questions, for those who have them, and finding answers that facilitate adaptation, may even be thought of as another task of mourning.

What makes the questions arise as they do? Where do they come from? What makes the human search for answers so intense, resulting quite often in strongly held beliefs despite scarce evidence in standard forms? For one thing, loss is so painful that mourners need whatever comfort they can find or imagine. We offer yet another hypothesis: The experience of death is so shocking that it brings forth new and more profound understandings of life. Loss teaches us a new lesson about life whether we are ready to learn or not.

This Lesson opened with a quotation from C.S. Lewis that ends: "She died. She is dead. Is the word so difficult to learn?" Lewis would undoubtedly have agreed that the word *death* and its meaning are indeed difficult to learn. Even very sensitive and thoughtful people can spend a lifetime not learning about death, putting it off, refusing to face it, eager to move on to almost any alternative topic or activity. Many parts of Western culture support a rather glib view of death as something natural that simply needs to be faced, along with a parallel devaluation of life. Turn on the evening news and learn in the most routine way of two more murders downtown, a life-destroying road accident, a natural disaster, a school shooting, and reports of casualties in another out-of-control war. Interspersed are ads for violent films and TV crime dramas. Those who have not experienced loss may not notice this almost casual approach to human life and death.

Those who mourn often have another view of life and death. The horror of death creates a new sensitivity to the importance of life. They are troubled by this casual approach to death, because they have learned something from loss that others may not understand: life is unbelievably and indescribably precious!

At death a life is finished, a person is gone, a being has been terminated. People who have experienced loss understand this, very often with a depth and sensitivity that others do not (yet) have. This is part of what makes the tasks of mourning so difficult. But a new opportunity is provided for learning from loss: an awakened awareness of how important, valuable, and irreplaceable human life is. What one learns from loss is not only the meaning of the word *death*, but the meaning of the word *life*. Is the word *life* so difficult to learn? Perhaps, yes, but learning the meaning of life seems to be the final and most important lesson for learning from loss.

DIALOGUE

Counselor: Did your first wife grow up in a religious tradition?

Mourner: Yes, she was active in the youth group in the small Congregational Church in the town where she was raised, and she became president of the statewide youth organization. She had strong spiritual beliefs about serenity and human kindness that evolved as she started teaching yoga and meditation later in her life.

Counselor: In what ways?

Mourner: She became unusually calm, as she was battling her cancer, and developed a following of students in her classes who came to regard her as a spiritual leader, a kind of guru. She had a quiet manner and a soft voice, making people so relaxed that they fell asleep at the end of the class.

Counselor: I can picture her. What did she think about death and an afterlife?

Mourner: I don't know because we didn't talk about it. I guess we thought she was doing so well that she wouldn't die. Maybe a little denial on our part.

Counselor: But you describe her as a spiritual leader with followers.

Mourner: She had a close friend who had become a kind of assistant who covered her classes during those last days. One day, knowing that death was coming, that person said to me, "She is at such an advanced state in her spiritual development, that she can no longer live here on earth. She is already in a higher spiritual realm, and she needs to be freed to go there, to a place where she will be more at home spiritually."

Counselor: And what did you think of that?

Mourner: I thought her friend knew a side of her from observing her in the classes that I didn't know as well. It opened my eyes to how people regarded her. Later in life, as I read about Buddhism, I wondered if she was a spiritual avatar, or would become one.

Counselor: That a rebirth might be possible?

Mourner: For her. Yes, possible.

Counselor: You were a Christian minister, briefly, but you seem to care about other world religions as well.

Mourner: Yes. I had excellent training in foundational methods in Biblical studies, but when I was working at the historically black college, I commuted to a nearby university and took half of a master's degree in world religions. I was also able to incorporate some further study of religion in my doctoral studies which left me with a life-long curiosity about world religions. But it was really my undergraduate liberal arts education that sparked my curiosity about nearly everything and left me with a mixture of awe and skepticism about timeless questions.

Counselor: And your handicapped daughter? Was she interested in religion?

Mourner: Yes. She studied theology and sang in church choirs as an opportunity for using her beautiful voice and employing her ability to learn new music quickly by ear. I couldn't help thinking when she died, many years after her mother died: Now if ever there was a candidate for reincarnation, she was it. She certainly deserved another opportunity to live life without being blind and physically handicapped.

Counselor: Do you think that could happen?

Mourner: How wise it was of those ancient Hindus to suggest rebirth. I always felt she deserved another chance. I like to imagine what she could have become without those disabilities. Getting blasted with meningitis on the first day of life! Doesn't that deserve a second chance? Oh. Hold on here for a minute. Could it happen? Are you asking me about my beliefs? I'm mostly filled with doubts, but I have a lot of hope. Hope doesn't rest on evidence. In fact, hope seems to emerge despite evidence. If strong hope is faith, I guess you can say I have some.

Counselor: Tell me more about the beliefs of your wife, your recent loss. I remember your telling me that you teased her about worshipping a sun god.

Mourner: Oh, yes, being from Brazil, she didn't care for winter, but she loved to soak up the summer sun when we would go walking in that wooded park that now has her memorial bench. I can see how people in ancient civilizations worshipped the sun, depending as they did on its warmth and power. But she was raised as a Catholic and as a teen and young adult she was close friends with a very scholarly and devoted priest.

Counselor: So she grew up with and continued to hold traditional Catholic beliefs?

Mourner: She was not a fan of the institutional church but said that she had her own private faith. She believed that her life was in God's hands and that she would be going on a journey to the afterlife. She was open to other ideas about religion, but she always came back to her core Catholic faith.

Counselor: She had a strong commitment then to a few cherished beliefs.

Mourner: Yes. She had a small, framed picture that she called "The Sacred Face" and she prayed to it each night. People will criticize that today, call it magic or something worse, but here's what I noticed: her faith made a huge difference in how she lived.

Counselor: In what ways?

Mourner: I think I told you that she lost her memory and seemed disoriented for six months at the end of her life. But she never lost faith, at least not as I observed her each day. She was calm, cooperative, still smiling, living her life as if she were still in God's hands, knew where she was going, and wasn't afraid.

Counselor: You could tell that by observing her?

Mourner: I think so. We didn't need to talk about it. She lived her faith, and it was inspiring to watch. In fact, I'm a bit awestruck admiring how bravely she faced death. I mean, it seems to make a difference, you know, when people trust in their God.

Counselor: So, you've been saying that her beliefs, whether regarded as true or not by others, made a difference in how she lived her life.

Mourner: That's what the field of psychology of religion seems to be telling us. And not just at the end of her life. She was always a very caring person, who thought about others, went out of her way to help people, even strangers. She lived the good life and appreciated every experience fully. And she was happy.

Counselor: Tell me more, then, about how you adjusted to life without her. It must have been very difficult.

Mourner: Well, now you can see what a terrible loss it was for me. As I mentioned before, we had that Remembrance Day for her, but looking back now, after reading about other observances, I wish I had done more to say good-bye. Much more.

Counselor: Such as…

Mourner: Beginning with her death. I wish I had been there that night to be with her. I just got a phone call the next morning to come over to the care facility before they took her body for cremation. It just seems like other cultures have better ways of saying goodbye, with more respect, more chance to be around their beloved. So, she was taken away and there I was alone.

Counselor: What effect did that have on you?

Mourner: It was alarming! I think the abruptness of it made me very disoriented. I've always struggled with the larger question of the meaning of life, but this loss really threw me into a tailspin. I think I told you that I just sobbed for weeks.

Counselor: So, would you say that you experienced some loss of meaning?

Mourner: In my personal life, yes, I was tired and unmotivated at first, and then I started to dwell on the pointless absurdity of life in general. Why are there so many billions of humans on this small planet, ruining it in new ways each day, at war with each other as nations and even within families? Why the prejudgments about anyone with the slightest bit of difference, including skin color, hair style, language, or sexual orientation? A devaluation of life itself, capped off with egocentric self-assertion. When she was alive, she kept me calm, walking me through all that absurd stuff, but when she died, I had to face it alone.

Counselor: What did you do? Or perhaps I should ask, what are you doing and does any of it work to help you restore meaning?

Mourner: Well, first of all, I decided I couldn't save the world, but there might be some small ways to be happy and relieve a little suffering here and there, like the Buddha taught—well, for that matter Jesus, Mohammed, and all the others, too. But what should I do? I was badly confused about that. I wish I had held a more formal memorial service for her, but as I mentioned before, many old friends, neighbors, and colleagues came to her Day of Remembrance, and from that day I began to rebuild my fragile social life and a new me. As I embraced their friendships, I was reminded of the person I was before I retired. So, I decided to return to an aspect of my former self and continue to write.

Counselor: And did that turn things around for you?

Mourner: A writing project came along, and I did well on that. Then I got the idea for a book on grief, something that might help mourners suffering a loss, but also providers of help. Suddenly, I had a lot to do, and as life went by around me, pointless and absurd, I had something to work on that felt important and meaningful. I also became committed to living like she lived, with or without her beliefs, but living each day as if I had her faith.

Counselor: Wow! That's inspiring. How do you keep motivated?

Mourner: One day, quite by accident, I found in the nightstand beside our bed—excuse me, my bed now—a small card with a message called "A Thought for Today." I recognized it as something we picked up at a Cistercian monastery, you know, where they take a vow of silence. It was near the town where my brother had lived and died. I had read it before, but now it seemed to have a new meaning. I carry it with me. May I read it to you?

Counselor: Yes, of course.

Mourner: It goes like this.

A Thought for Today

This is the beginning of a new day. God has
given this day to use as I will. I can waste it,
or use it for good. What I do today is important
because I'm exchanging a day of my life for it.
When tomorrow comes, this day will be gone forever,
leaving in its place something I have traded for it.
I want it to be gain, not loss; good, not evil;
success, not failure; in order that I shall not regret
the price I paid for it.

—Abbey of Genesee
Piffard, New York

Mourner: I'm sorry. I still find myself fighting off tears when I am reading that out loud.

Counselor: You were together when you came upon it at the Abbey?

Mourner: Yes, that's part of it, but it's so beautiful, and it makes me wonder how I can find life to be meaningful after such a terrible loss. I know that A Thought for Today is full of high expectations and the people I show it to think it is too stern, too monastic, but I know that it fuels my motivation.

Counselor: Perhaps they are concerned that there's no time to smell the roses or sip a hot tea by a warm fire on a cold day.

Mourner: Yes, but I don't look at those things as time-wasting. Those are moments well spent, too. To me, A Thought for the Day is the supreme statement of how precious life is. Think of it: I'm exchanging a day of my life for whatever I do with it. Then that day is gone, and I'm left with whatever I've done. If I'm lucky, I might just get one more day to walk the lonely path, so I best not waste it.

Counselor: I guess that's turning a life that could be pointless and absurd into something priceless and precious. I'm noticing you're twisting around in your seat. Are you searching for something?

Mourner: Always. Right now, I'm looking for that clock you have on the wall behind me here. Oh, I see my time is up.

Counselor: For today.

REFERENCES

Davis, J. (2022). *Timeless Questions: How World Religions Explore the Mysteries of Life*. Santa Fe, NM: Sunstone Press.

DeVine, M. (2017). *It's OK That You're Not OK*. Boulder, CO: Sounds True.

Hinnells, J. Ed. (2012). *The Penguin Handbook of the World's Living Religions*. New York: Penguin Books.

Kessler, D. (2019). *Finding Meaning: The Sixth Stage of Grief*. New York: Simon & Schuster.

Malkinson, R. (2007). *Cognitive Grief Therapy: Constructing a Rational Meaning to Life Following Loss*. New York: W.W. Norton & Company.

Moffat, M.J. (1992). *In the Midst of Winter: Selections from the Literature of Mourning*. New York: Random House.

Parkes, C.M., Laungani, P., and Young, B. (2015). *Death and Bereavement Across Cultures*. Second Edition. New York: Routledge.

Pelikan, J. (1990). *The World Treasury of Modern Religious Thought*. Boston: Little, Brown, and Company.

Rockwell, W. (2006). *The Utes: A Forgotten People*. Montrose, CO: Western Reflections Publishing.

Thoreau, H.D. (1982). *Walden and Other Writings*. New York: Bantam Books. Originally published in 1854.

Worden, J.W. (2018). *Grief Counseling and Grief Therapy: A Handbook for Mental Health Practitioners*, Fifth Edition. New York: Springer Publishing.

ANNOTATED BIBLIOGRAPHY

Eleven Important Resources

A review of the literature on grief, which was begun online with lists recommended by therapists, led to an acquaintance with various types of books on grief. (See Preface.) After careful perusal and extensive reading, the books identified as most helpful were eventually reduced to the following list of eleven. Although we would not claim to have done an exhaustive search or to have located every important book on grief (some recognized works may be missing), we have identified what we believe is a sufficient list of key resources for the writing of this book. Naturally, important topics overlap and appear in more than one work, but each reference on our list, we believe, in some way makes a unique contribution to the specific purposes of the book we chose to write. Brief descriptions of those contributions are included here.

Bonanno, G.A. (2019). *The Other Side of Sadness: What the New Science of Bereavement Tells about Life After Loss.* New York: Basic Books.

Resilience is a central theme in this work, supporting descriptions in Lesson 3 of what resilience is and why it is a more likely result of mourning as compared with prolonged grief. This book also contains interesting summaries of mourning practices in other cultures as described in Lesson 5.

DeVine, M. (2017). *It's OK That You're Not OK.* Boulder, CO: Sounds True.

The author's personal loss is the basis of her own grief as she describes a culturally shaped reluctance to listen to, acknowledge, and understand the deep sadness of mourning. This work, cited in several Lessons, helps readers to see that it is okay (normal) to have intense feelings of sadness not easily addressed or resolved.

Hagman, G. (Ed.) (2016). *New Models of Bereavement, Theory, and Treatment*. New York: Routledge.

This edited volume contains many interesting chapters by various scholars, including an insightful Introduction by Robert A. Neimeyer. The work contains an especially valuable chapter by the editor, George Hagman, on the concept of "self," and how the self is damaged and rebuilt through grief, as explained in Lesson 4.

Kessler, D. (2019). *Finding Meaning: The Sixth Stage of Grief*. New York: Simon & Schuster.

This book is a source on stage theory, but its main focus is on making meaning through various ways of memorializing the deceased as described in Lesson 4.

Malkinson, R. (2007). *Cognitive Grief Therapy: Constructing a Rational Meaning to Life Following Loss*. New York: W.W. Norton.

This work provides a comprehensive explanation of the foundational principles of cognitive therapy as presented in Lesson 3. It is the source of valuable concepts such as the ABC Model, self-talk, and cognitive control.

Moffat, M.J. (1992). *In the Midst of Winter: Selections from the Literature of Mourning*. New York: Random House.

The short quotations of literary prose and poetry found intermittently across all five Lessons are drawn from this excellent anthology of classic writing about grief. The carefully selected materials represent many genres, types of authors, and time periods. Moffat has gained permissions for inclusion in her work and has listed them at the beginning. We use only a few lines from each selection, within fair use guidelines, but we identify each original source and the page reference as cited in Moffat.

Nieburgh. and Fischer, A. (1982). *Pet Loss.* New York: Harper & Row.

Brief mentions of pet loss are based on this useful work that demonstrates the parallels between grief for the loss of a pet and human grief processes, as described in Lesson 3.

O'Connor, M-F. (2022). *The Grieving Brain.* New York: Harper Collins Publishers.

This recently published work contains some of the latest findings of the emerging field of neuroscience and includes explanations of the implications of this research for grief. Insights from this work appear in Lessons 2 and 4.

Parkes, C.M., Laungani, P., and Young, B. (2015). *Death and Bereavement Across Cultures.* Second Edition. New York: Routledge.

This excellent source on religious beliefs and mourning practices of other cultures provides a basis for the discussion in Lesson 5.

Rando, T. (1991). *How to Go on Living When Someone You Love Dies.* New York: Bantam Books.

This work serves as a parallel and supplemental source to others on the mediators of grief, including type of relationship and manner of death. It contains information similar to that drawn from J.W, Worden in Lesson 1. It is also a useful source of grief activities and contains a list of available agencies and resources at the time of its publication.

Worden, J.W. (2018). *Grief Counseling and Grief Therapy: A Handbook for Mental Health Practitioners,* Fifth Edition. New York: Springer Publishing.

This is a comprehensive textbook on grief therapy and has been drawn on frequently for definitions, historical perspectives, foundational concepts, and research on grief. It is the source for the four tasks of grief used as an organizing structure for Lessons 2, 3, and 4. Its inclusion of key concepts and reported research findings makes it a highly respected reference on grief. It is our most frequently used scholarly resource and is cited throughout all five Lessons.

AUTHOR'S BOOK

Listed separately, because it is not a book on grief and is written by one of the authors, James R. Davis, this work is drawn upon for sections in Lesson 5 on life after death, the meaning of life, and the good life. In that lesson an interdisciplinary perspective is introduced, not usually found in other books on grief.

Davis, J. (2022). *Timeless Questions: How World Religions Explore the Mysteries of Life*. Santa Fe, NM: Sunstone Press.

This book is used as a key reference in Lesson 5 for exploring what world religions say about the timeless questions that address the "existential quest for meaning." This source is used freely without reference since the material is under the author's own copyright. Although many works describing the world religions are referred to in this work, the following are of special importance to Lesson 5 and are acknowledged here.

Aslan, R. (2011). *No god but God: The Origins, Evolution, and Future of Islam*. New York: Random House.

Bashkarananda, S. (2002). *The Essentials of Hinduism*. Seattle: Viveka Press.

Collins, J. (2004). *Introduction to the Hebrew Bible*. Minneapolis: Fortress Press.

Erdman. B. (2016). *The New Testament: An Historical Introduction*. Sixth Edition. New York: Oxford University Press.

Harris, I. (Ed.) (2011). *The Complete Illustrated Encyclopedia of Buddhism: A Comprehensive Guide to Buddhist History, Philosophy, and Practice*. Wigston, England: Hermes House of Annes Press.

Rainey, L.D. (2010). *Confucius & Confucianism: The Essentials*. Malden, MA: Wiley-Blackwell.

Rainey, L.D. (2014). *Decoding Dao: Reading the Dao De Jing and the Zhuangzi*. New York: John Wiley & Sons.

ABOUT THE AUTHORS

JAMES R. DAVIS is Professor and Dean Emeritus of the University of Denver, where he served as professor of higher education and adult studies, teaching graduate courses and advising doctoral students on their dissertation research. While doing this, he also held several administrative positions, including Director of the School of Education, Director of Faculty Development, and Dean of University College, the adult education graduate college. He holds the A.B. degree in history from Oberlin College, the B.D. degree in pastoral studies from Yale University Divinity School, and the PhD degree in higher education administration from Michigan State University. He is the author of eight academic books on college teaching, training, leadership, and interdisciplinary studies. Although most of his academic and administrative career was spent at the University of Denver, prior to that, he served for six years as a teacher and academic dean at historically black Wilberforce University (HBCU) in Ohio during the Civil Rights Movement. He also served as visiting lecturer at Yale University Divinity School. His academic interest in grief developed in retirement and as a result of his many losses, described in detail in the Dialogue sections of this book.

JULIE DAVIS ROBINSON is the adult daughter of James Davis. She is a registered clinical psychologist, currently practicing independently in Calgary, in the Province of Alberta, Canada. She holds the B.A. degree in psychology from the University of Denver, where she graduated summa cum laude. She continued her studies and earned the Doctor of Psychology (PsyD) degree in clinical psychology at the University of Denver's School of Professional Psychology. After her internship at Alberta Children's Hospital, she worked there briefly before entering private practice with special interests in child, adolescent, and young adult counseling. She is a member of the College of Alberta Psychologists (CAP) and Psychologist's Association of Alberta (PAA). An enthusiastic advocate of "walk-and-talk" therapy, she continued her practice through the pandemic in this way. Julie experienced early loss of her mother to lymphoma two weeks before her high school graduation, as described in the Dialogue sections of this book.

READERS GUIDE

1. Most books on grief suggest that "all grief is different." In Lesson 1, we learn to describe *how* it is different and what the mediating factors are that impact each loss. In what ways would you say that your grief is unique? What are the strongest influences affecting your grief?

2. In Lesson 2, we identify three stories to be told: the backstory, the event story, and the impact story. Have you found someone to whom you can tell these stories? If so, which story was the most difficult to tell?

3. Which feelings, physical responses, and thought patterns were most prominent to you in the early days and weeks of mourning? Which were most troublesome?

4. In Lesson 3, we provide a comprehensive list of things to try that might help with your grieving. Have you tried any of them? Which ones were most helpful and why? Can you suggest others?

5. Of the many external adjustments (housing, childcare, domestic roles, etc.) which ones have you had to make? Of these, which was the most challenging?

6. What aspects of the self were most impacted by this loss? How entwined were your lives, and what part of your self seems to be missing now?

7. Are you beginning to experience resilience, and do you want to build a new life? What part of that challenge is most difficult? What aspects of your former self are you using as a foundation for a new life?

8. What place do continuing bonds, memories, and memorials have in your new life? In what ways does your loved one still have a presence in your life?

9. What spiritual issues are you dealing with now, and are you rethinking certain beliefs and practices? How are you making meaning and what type of good life are you trying to live?

10. The Dialogues between **Mourner** and **Counselor** illustrate the ideas in each lesson but also the qualities of an expert listener. Have you found one or more skilled listeners? Could you become a skilled listener now for someone who has experienced loss?

www.ingramcontent.com/pod-product-compliance
Lightning Source LLC
Chambersburg PA
CBHW012303240726
48656CB00008B/2516